ever after

ever after

life lessons learned in my castle of chaos

vicki courtney

B&H
PUBLISHING GROUP

Nashville, Tennessee

Published by B&H Publishing Group
Nashville, Tennessee

Dewey Decimal Classification: 248.843
Subject Heading: MOTHERHOOD \ MARRIAGE \
WOMEN

Author is represented by Alive Communications, Inc., 7680
Goddard Street, Suite 200, Colorado Springs, CO 80920.

1 2 3 4 5 6 7 8 • 17 16 15 14 13

To Keith

I was the little girl who wholeheartedly believed the fairy tales when they said that someday, my prince would come. What I love best about our story is that you showed up on the same exact day I met my one, Prince, Jesus Christ. You were there for that moment and witnessed the first page being turned in a new chapter of my life. From that day forward, you have been faithful to point me in His direction—to the only one who could truly complete me. What a blessed girl I am.

Contents

Acknowledgments ix

Introduction 1

Chapter 1   House Sweet Home 7

Chapter 2   Prince Charming Letdown 21

Chapter 3   P-31 Flunkie 37

Chapter 4   Save the Date .51

Chapter 5   Unmet Sexpectations 65

Chapter 6   Duty or Desire? 79

Chapter 7   Repeat after Me: NO 93

Chapter 8   Quitting the Family Busyness 107

Chapter 9   Water with Lemon 121

Chapter 10 School Daze 131

Chapter 11 Circle the Bandwagons 141

Chapter 12 Merry Christmas from the
            Stepford Family 153

Chapter 13 Hold on Loosely 167

Chapter 14 I Love Me; I Love Me Not 181

Chapter 15 Fine Whines: Aged to Perfection 197

Chapter 16 Happily-Ever-After 209

Acknowledgments

K eith, I often wonder if you had been given a tiny glimpse of what exactly you were signing up for on that day we stood at the altar about twenty-five years ago and exchanged "I do's," if you would have run for the hills and never looked back. Wow, what an adventure. And a good one, at that. Thank you for allowing me to talk about our fairy tale in a very public forum—I wouldn't trade a single detail for where we are today. I am so excited to spend the next twenty-five years (and more!) with my very best friend.

Ryan (and Casey), Paige (and Matt), and Hayden, thank you for allowing me the freedom to talk about the behind-the-scenes moments in the life of our family. We are not perfect; but, praise God, we are perfectly forgiven.

Thank you to my amazing publisher, B&H. I cannot begin to express my gratitude for your partnership over the past ten years. It's been a tremendous honor to be a part of your family. Now, and always.

Lee (a.k.a. best literary agent in the universe), you amaze me. Truly, amaze me. I've thought of you so often while writing this book. No one expects their fairy tale to include a diagnosis of brain cancer. The words fairy tale and cancer don't even belong in the same sentence. You are a living testimony that happily-ever-after is not the result of circumstances, but rather our relationship with the Lord. I'm proud to be on your team of prayer warriors.

Thank you to the many women who, over the years, shared your own stories of fairy-tale expectations that didn't quite measure up to reality. Your testimonies have greatly influenced my desire to write this book.

And above all, thank you to my Lord and Savior, Jesus Christ. I grew up believing that "someday, my prince will come." You swept me off my feet on August 30, 1985, and I have yet to recover from it. I pray I never do. You are the love of my life, my one true Prince, and the source of my happily-ever-after.

Life itself is the most wonderful fairy tale.

~HANS CHRISTIAN ANDERSEN

Introduction

Once upon a time, there was a little girl who loved a good fairy tale. Oh, not just *any* fairy tale, mind you. The Cinderella-meets-her-Prince-Charming kind of fairy tale. (Minus of course, the evil stepmother, stepsister drama, and chimney-sweeping gig.) Like most other princesses in waiting, her heart was drawn to the handsome prince, ornately decorated castle, and especially, the happily-ever-after that was sealed with a kiss. Bonus points for the personal attendants that were part of the postkiss wedding package. This little girl got older and eventually outgrew the classic fairy tales, but the happily-ever-after expectation remained. She satisfied her fairy-tale appetite with chick flicks, romance novels, and late-night girl talk sessions where she and her posse of best girlfriends mastered the art of overanalyzing the motives of their latest crushes. The princess and her friends had been raised to believe that someday their princes would come. White horse, chariot, or trendy sports car—the means of transportation didn't matter as long as he arrived on the scene in a timely manner and could spare them the shame of a closet full of useless bridesmaid dresses. Or worse yet, a constant barrage of reminders from their mothers about their ticking biological clocks.

The princess went off to college, and after dating more than a few toads, her prince finally arrived. While attending a Christian weekend retreat for college students, the princess locked eyes with a handsome young fellow who had "future prince" written all over him. True to her fairy-tale expectations, it was love at first sight. Well, at least for the princess. The prince apparently had failed to read the script and missed the love-at-first-sight cue. Oh, but that's not all. In the days following the retreat, he called and asked for the phone number of one of the princess's friends, so he could ask her to his law school formal. A tiny diversion from the princess's imagined script, but alas, love cannot be rushed. For the record, that sweet princess may or may not have given the prince the wrong phone number before hanging up the phone and sobbing into her pillow for the next half hour. Where was that wand-waving fairy when you needed her? Clearly, Cinderella was staying home from the law school ball.

One year later, those tears were long forgotten when the princess glanced down at the beautiful diamond solitaire on her left hand. She may have missed out on accompanying the prince to his law school formal, but she would be on his arm at the only ball that really mattered. Her prince had finally come, and the fairy-tale life she had dreamed about was about to begin. Or so she thought. Unfortunately, the chick flicks, romance novels, and sappy love songs ended where real life began. Where was the scene, chapter, or song lyric about the prince playing in a softball tournament on the day they brought their first baby home from the hospital? (Oh, yes he did!) Or the one where the princess talked the prince into buying a "castle" they couldn't afford? Where is the scene, chapter, or song lyric detailing the pain of raising a rebellious teenager? Or the one where their family became a slave to a calendar of nonstop activities and their faith sometimes got lost in the shuffle? Or how about the one where they eventually found themselves sitting in a counselor's office wondering what in the world had become of the prince/princess they thought they had married years before? Juggling marriage and motherhood was much harder than the princess had imagined. A wand-waving fairy would have been helpful in moments like this. And much cheaper.

Twenty-five years have gone by since the princess and the prince began their very own fairy-tale adventure. Their children are grown and have left the nest. They stop by to visit often, but they don't stay overnight. Their rooms are clean.

Their beds stay made. There are fewer loads of laundry and less junk food in the pantry. The sibling rivalry has ceased. The house is quiet. Sometimes, eerily quiet. The prince and the princess have more time for each other, and while they miss the chapters where the children were younger, they don't want to turn back the pages and live them all over again. They go on dates often and take trips. They spend time with their friends. They even stay up late on some weekends, without a single worry of whether or not that teenager will make curfew. They are enjoying this new chapter and, especially, the blessing that comes with being their children's friends.

On this particular morning, the princess sits in her tidy family room and ponders these things. The fairy tale didn't quite pan out as she had imagined. She smiles at that thought. If she learned anything from the fairy tale, it's that real life happens behind the scenes. It was in the struggles, the messiness, the imperfections that the princess discovered herself and, more importantly, the God who created her. And that is far better than the classic fairy tale. Juggling the responsibilities that came with marriage, motherhood, and managing the home front was exhausting on most days. It was the hardest thing she has ever done but also one of her greatest achievements. On most days, she fell into her bed at night and wondered if she would ever feel like she was giving *enough*. Enough to her husband. Enough to her children. Enough to her God. Over the years, she would compare herself to other women who seemed to have it all together. In truth, they too were collapsing into their beds at night and wondering if they were giving enough.

Sure, she made mistakes along the way. If she could go back, she might do some things differently. As she opens her Bible on this quiet morning, she realizes that she is who she is today because of those messier behind-the-scenes moments that defined her fairy tale. Those were the moments that made her cling to an all-knowing, always consistent, and ever-patient God. He had her back during those years. He carried her through it all and gave her the strength she needed to make it through each day. And more importantly, he carried her husband and children, as well. He taught them all valuable lessons in those not-so-fairy-tale moments of life. And in that moment, the princess wished for one thing. She wished she could go back and tell her younger princess-self, *Let it go. Lighten up. Go easier on yourself. I know the ending to this fairy tale, and I can tell you this: Everything is going to be OK. Better than you ever hoped or imagined.*

And with that thought, the princess realized the moral to her fairy tale: God's grace is always enough. While she couldn't go back and remind her younger princess-self of that amazing truth, maybe, just maybe, he would allow her to remind the sweet princesses who were just steps behind her in the journey. The tired ones. The discouraged ones. Yes, the ones who collapse into their beds at night and wonder if they will ever feel like they are giving enough. She would tell them that with God it is more than *enough* and encourage them to claim that truth now. In *this* chapter of their lives.

Ever After is a result of that princess's prayer on that quiet morning. It is my story. My fairy tale, if you will. The backstage moments. The life lessons. The chaos. The laughter. And yes, even the tears. It is my prayer that *Ever After* will be the hug of encouragement you need as you are juggling the challenges that come with marriage and motherhood. *Happily-ever-after* is not a storybook ending that only happens in fictional fairy tales. It is possible today. Your Prince has come. Your *happily-ever-after* awaits.

Chapter 1

House Sweet Home

Every princess wants a castle. Maybe that desire stems from the fairy-tale indoctrination that begins at an early age, but a castle or, better yet, a dream house is part of the happily-ever-after equation. We want a place to call our own, a place where we can put our mark and style in the rooms and make it uniquely ours. No fairy tale is complete without a castle.

While recently going though a box of old photos my mother had given me, I found a picture of me and several of the neighbor kids on the back porch, playing "house" under a patio table covered by several sheets. I couldn't have been older than about three or four years old, yet it was clear that I was the matriarch of the card-table castle. I had one of my mother's purses slung over my shoulder and wore a pair of dress-up high heels as I hoisted a baby doll on my hip. A neighbor boy with an indignant expression stood beside me in the picture. It was clear he had been recruited to play the assigned role of the breadwinning patriarch and was none too happy about it. My mother told me that I even made the poor fellow kiss me shortly after the picture was snapped—right before I shooed him off to his pretend job. Even as a child, I recognized the importance of a home (albeit an unsteady one) to raise my pretend children and fulfill my fairy-tale destiny.

Within a couple of years, I upgraded the card-table castle for something a bit fancier. While playing at a neighbor friend's house one afternoon, I walked into her room and was greeted by the most beautiful dream house I'd ever laid eyes on: Barbie's Dream Townhouse (vintage 1970s). Her house had an elevator, for heaven's sake. And after catching an eyeful of that handsome Ken fellow, the neighbor boy was off the hook of playing the role of the handsome prince. My Barbie-loving neighbor friend and I would script scene after scene of imaginary fun, all the while living vicariously through our girl, Barbie.

Barbie's life was so simple. Get up and put on terry cloth bathrobe and fuzzy slippers. Take the tiny elevator down to the dream kitchen and heat up a miniature plate of plastic goodness. After breakfast, lounge on the sofa and watch TV (though the channel seemed to have only one station). No mom around to nag Barbie about doing her chores or getting ready for school on time. She was free to hop in her pink Corvette and meet her friend, Midge, for a quick game of tennis whenever she so desired. After tennis, it was back to the townhouse to get ready for a hot date with her beau, Ken.

Getting Barbie ready for her dream date could take up countless hours of fun as we sorted through her extensive wardrobe in search of the perfect outfit. Once she was ready, Ken would pull up in his safari Jeep and knock on the door of Barbie's dream house. When she opened the door, he was clearly wowed by her elaborate evening gown with a matching fur stole (PETA friendly, of course). Who wouldn't want that life? Or at the very least, her town house and closet full of clothes?!

Real-Life Castles

Even as a child, I knew that castles belonged in fairy tales. That is, until I was a teenager and my friends and I caught wind of a real-life fairy tale in the making. Along with 750 million viewers, we set our alarm clocks and woke up in the early morning hours to catch the live coverage of Lady Diana Spencer, a shy kindergarten teacher, as she wed Charles, the Prince of Wales. I was mesmerized when I saw Diana emerge princess-style from an ornate carriage and make her way into

St. Paul's Cathedral with her twenty-five-foot train trailing elegantly behind her. My friends and I oohed and aahed over her stunning bridal gown with a ruffled neckline and '80s puffed sleeves.

After growing up on a steady diet of animated fairy tales, this was as close as it gets when it comes to a real-life fairy tale. During the wedding ceremony, the Archbiship of Canterbury said, "Here is the stuff of which fairy tales are made." And we all believed him. One scene that will forever stay etched in my memory took place after the wedding when the prince and princess stepped out onto the balcony of Buckingham Palace and waved to the crowd of 250,000 cheering onlookers. If my friends and I were impressed with the dress, seeing the palace wowed us even more. She would live in the palace until her own castle was ready.

As you know, there would be no happily-ever-after ending to this fairy tale. The custom wood-carved furniture, marble statues, and perfectly manicured private gardens could not save their marriage. Perhaps, their divorce should have been our first clue that happy marriages must be about more than dream castles and perfect princes. Yet the fairy-tale dream continues. We want to believe there is a prince who will come for us. We want the romance, the engagement, and all that comes with it. After we get the ring, we want to take our prince to the local Bed Bath & Beyond, grab one of those registry scanner guns, and zap up a wish list of goodies for our future castle. We want the twenty-four-piece Calphalon cookware set, the stainless flatware, monogrammed bath towels, and four-hundred-count Egyptian cotton bedsheets. Setting up our future homes is part of the fairy-tale dream.

A Place to Call Home

When my husband carried me over the threshold of our first castle, I could hardly wait to begin our new life together. For the record, our "castle" was a seven-hundred-square-foot apartment with laminate countertops, sketchy-looking carpet, and a lovely view of the parking lot below. I guess you could call it a starter castle. Regardless, it felt like home sweet home and I was anxious to begin the first chapter of the fairy tale I'd dreamed about since I was a little girl. I settled in my mind that the real castle would come later.

Honestly, those first couple of months of wedded bliss felt a lot like playing house. I baked dinner for my husband and served it on our new dishes. I made pies from scratch and even wore a sweet calico apron I had received at a wedding shower. If I was going to burn something in the kitchen, at least I looked good doing it. Life for a family of two was fairly simple. Keith was working full-time and I was finishing up my final semester of college, so we had time to enjoy newlywed life. The fairy tale was off to a good start, except for one small detail: the castle walls were beginning to close in on me. Some of our couple friends were upgrading their apartments to starter homes and I caught the bug to upgrade our digs. I had a serious case of castle envy.

By my one-year anniversary, I would have a starter home (and a baby on the way). We would go through a couple more castles before we settled into the castle we currently live in today. We've owned our current castle for nearly two decades and if I have it my way, my husband and I will grow old together in it. When we moved into this house, our two older children were about to begin first grade and preschool, and our youngest child had just taken his first baby steps. I raised my kids in this castle and it has served as the launchpad for all three of my children as they've made their way into the world.

It wasn't long ago that my oldest son spent his last night in his childhood bedroom before catching a flight the following day to Huntsville, Alabama, to marry his wife. Not long after, my daughter would spend her last night in her childhood bedroom before marrying her husband. And just recently, I hugged my youngest child good-bye on the driveway before he climbed into his truck packed-to-the-brim with his belongings and headed about ten miles down the road to begin his second year of college at the University of Texas.

I've got this drop-off drill down, so I didn't expect to shed any tears. For the record, this was college drop-off #10, so I've had plenty of practice. Not to mention, I knew I would see the boy the next day when I stopped by to make his bed and help him tidy up his new apartment. I was a tower of strength when I hugged him good-bye on the driveway. But something within me shifted when I watched him back out and make his way down the street with his belongings strapped in the back bed of his truck. What happened? Wasn't it just yesterday that he was zipping around on his Big Wheel on this very same driveway while I sat on a lawn chair making a grocery list as he and his siblings played? Castles are important to mothers because they serve as the backdrop for many forever memories.

As I watched my boy leave for college that day, I thanked God through happy tears for giving me a dream home rather than a dream house. There's a difference, you know. When we first moved into our home, I continued to struggle with "castle envy." If I walked into a friend's home and it was bigger, fancier, or more updated, I would leave feeling dissatisfied. I would walk back into my home and see the stains on the carpet, the outdated mini-blinds on the windows, and my poor, pathetic entertainment center from Sam's Club. Would there ever come a day when I could replace the carpet with wood floors, dress the windows up with real drapes, or own a piece of furniture made out of real wood?

In the early years, I bought into the lie that granite countertops, stainless appliances, and well-appointed rooms with a perfect palette of paint colors splashed on the walls would bring happiness and fulfillment. Even if I got those things, it was only a matter of time before I would relapse into another episode of castle envy. I recall one particular occasion many years ago when I picked one of my kids up at a friend's house. The home was in a beautiful neighborhood with breathtaking views of the hill country and even one of the nearby lakes in Austin. As I exited the neighborhood, I stopped my car in front of a home with a real estate sign on the front lawn and grabbed the information sheet out of curiosity. After seeing the price tag, I began to mentally calculate whether or not we could afford the home. The monthly payment was well above what we were paying at the time, but then I found myself adding in the amount of our monthly tithe to our church. Like I could ever talk my godly husband into that one! I'm ashamed to say that I even considered it before coming to my senses and snapping out of yet another episode of castle envy.

Over the years I've learned that there will always be houses bigger than mine, cleaner than mine, and more well-appointed than mine. If I get caught up in the comparison trap of always wanting what I don't have, I miss the joy of appreciating what I do have. Once I realized that dream houses don't always translate into dream homes, I was able to see my house through a different filter. We alone determine whether or not our houses will be homes. And we will pass that attitude onto our children.

Dream Houses and Dream Homes

I've watched the dream house phenomenon play out on Pinterest. Women have devoted entire pinboards to their home-decorating inspirations. I have one myself, but I have to be careful that it doesn't cause me to suffer a relapse of castle envy. When I see beautifully decorated rooms that in theory would look amazing in my home, I have to stop, take a breath, and remind myself of the lesson I've learned about the difference between dream houses and dream homes.

Dream houses are built to impress those who live on the outside more than those who live on the inside. Dream houses are more about show and less about comfort. They are not always friendly to little children who are eventually bound to spill Kool-Aid on the expensive living room rug or ram their Tonka truck into the mahogany legs of the coffee table. Over and over again. Dream houses showcase fancy art on the walls rather than children's masterpieces on the refrigerator. They can look warm and cozy on the outside but feel chilly on the inside. Dream houses have a beautiful carpet of green grass on the front lawn where little children's bare feet are rarely allowed to tread. Dream houses are beautiful to look at but not always pleasant to live in.

Dream homes, on the other hand, have living rooms that are lived in and furniture that is comfortable. Dream homes are places where the neighbor kids gather to play because they are always welcome. They have walls with tiny handprint smudges and kitchens with sticky floors and doggie noseprints on the storm door. Dream homes have garages that store sports equipment, bikes, and all other manner of riding toys but rarely the family cars. They have dinner tables where family members sit for a meal and talk about their day. Dream homes have chair cushions that have been flipped over to hide the scribble marks from the toddler who got into his older sister's craft box. Dream homes have squeaky ceiling fans from little boys who thought it would be fun to see how far their stuffed animals would fly if tossed into the blades. They have Lego pieces under the sofa cushions and stickers on the bathroom mirror.

The most important distinguishing difference between dream houses and dream homes can be found in the foundation. Dream homes are built on a foundation of faith. Matthew 6:19–21 reminds us, "Do not lay up for yourselves treasures on earth, where moth and rust destroy and where thieves break in and steal, but lay up for yourselves treasures in heaven, where neither moth nor rust destroys and where thieves do not break in and steal. For where your treasure is, there your heart will be also" (ESV).

This passage is not saying it's wrong to have nice things in our homes. Rather, these verses are making a statement about the order of our priorities. Do we put more time and energy into filling our homes with things that will perish or memories that will last? Do we treat the Lord as a regular member of our household or an occasional visitor that is only welcome when invited? If the walls could talk, would they tell stories of open Bibles and bedtime prayers or Bibles with dusty covers grabbed on the way out the door on an occasional Sunday morning? Would they talk about the laughter shared around the dinner table or meals eaten alone in front of a TV or computer? Would they say that the Lord's name was spoken often or uttered in vain? Would they share about raised voices and slammed doors or sinners who lose their temper, but are quick to apologize and ask for forgiveness?

A Solid Foundation

Homes are only meant to provide shelter from the outside elements. A foundation of faith can be built in any home where a willing heart is present. A physical place to hang pictures on the wall and call our own is a bonus. Here is a frightening question to ponder: if our homes were to be suddenly destroyed by fire or storm, would we still have everything we need? Note that I said *need* and not *want* because there is a great distinction between the two. Many who have lost their homes have learned the hard way that there is a big difference between perceived needs and actual needs. If faced with the choice of physical shelter or the one true shelter from the storms of life, which would you choose? I'd rather live in a homeless shelter with Jesus than a mansion where he is not present.

For where your treasure is, there your heart will be also.

Dream homes exist in every neighborhood and all price ranges. Dream homes shelter flawed people who are more concerned with remodeling their hearts than their kitchens. They are safe havens to confess shortcomings rather than pretending they don't exist. Dream homes see their fair share of tears and heartaches, but the tears and heartaches are never faced alone. My children had the privilege of growing up in a dream home because their mother realized the difference between a dream house and a dream home before it was too late.

Even so, I will always struggle on some level with castle envy. While in the process of writing this chapter, I received the monthly edition of *Austin Elegant Living* (a free sales periodical that comes in the mail) and began thumbing through it. By page ten, I wanted to replace my garage door with one of those fancy wood ones, redo my master bath, and replace my wood spindles on my staircase with ornate iron ones. You get the picture. I know my limits, and thumbing through the remainder of the magazine would have launched me into a full-blown episode of castle envy. I closed the magazine and reached for my One Year Bible instead.

When I opened my Bible to the designated reading for the day, would you believe it was out of Ecclesiastes? You might remember Ecclesiastes—a book written by King Solomon and his quest for the meaning of life. In my daily reading, I read that King Solomon "denied [him]self no pleasure" (2:10 NLT) and that as part of his quest, he "tried to find meaning by building huge homes" (2:4 NLT). In the end, he concluded that "it was all meaningless—like chasing the wind" (2:11 NLT). But it was this bit of timely wisdom that offered just the remedy I needed: "Enjoy what you have rather than desiring what you don't have. Just dreaming about nice things is meaningless— like chasing the wind" (Eccles. 6:9 NLT). I'm pretty sure God staged an intervention that morning to remind me of some important truths that I need to meditate on often.

Dream homes come and go, but godly legacies are built on a foundation of faith. The sobering reality is that someday my husband and I will be gone. Our children will divvy up the contents of our dream home, slap a "for sale" sign in the front lawn, and sell it to the highest bidder. We can't take it with us, and that's mighty fine with me.

Chapter 2

Prince Charming Letdown

"A woman's heart should be so close to God that
a man should have to chase Him to find her."

~C. S. LEWIS

M ost every girl would admit to wanting the fairy tale—
the prince, the castle, and eventually the laughter of
little royal offspring echoing through the castle corridors. We
can blame it on chick flicks, romance novels, or our mothers
(who, by default of being our mothers, get blamed for most

everything). Oh sure, we are a product of our environment, but I also believe we enter the world hardwired to want the fairy tale. The Disney movies, chick flicks, and sappy song lyrics play on that internal desire to live happily-ever-after.

What girl doesn't remember dreaming about her Prince Charming? In my treasure trove of keepsakes, I have a note my daughter wrote me when she was seven years old. It was a checklist of qualities her future prince would have. She wrote: "Someday, I will marry a man who (a) is a cristen (I'm pretty sure she meant "Christian") (b) has blue eyes (c) is a Longhorn." Item "c" is a reference" to The University of Texas mascot. My daughter comes from a long line of Longhorns, and the college football brainwashing began at birth in our home. Never mind that the child ended up going to Auburn University.

My daughter recently married, and I'm happy to report that she did, in fact, marry a "cristen." For the record, he has green eyes and graduated from Auburn University. And thanks to a quality education, my daughter can finally spell "Christian." Oh well, if my son-in-law was going to match up on only one-third of my daughter's fairy tale wish list, at least he got the most important one right. He is a fine "cristen" young man, and I couldn't be more proud. Now that he lives in Texas, he's even open to rooting for the Longhorns. There's hope for him yet.

Most of us have a story to answer the question, "How did you know your husband was 'The One'?" We love the romantic details and hearing about our friends' "aha moments." But the "how we met" stories are nothing compared to the proposal stories. The motto nowadays seems to be "think big or go home." Girls today expect nothing short of a proposal that will become a viral YouTube sensation minutes after the question is popped. Anyone can get on one knee and say those magical yet predictable words, "Will you marry me?" Why not take it up a notch and hire the local high school marching band and enlist help from half the town to help you out with an impromptu flash-mob proposal? Oh wait, that one's already been done. Never mind.

The proposal is an important detail because it officially jumpstarts the fairy tale. Back in my day, it signaled that magical moment when you could go out and buy a half a dozen bridal magazines and begin dog-earing the pages that had dream wedding potential. Girls today often don't wait for a proposal and a ring to begin dreaming and planning for a wedding. While recently surfing around on the popular website Pinterest, I couldn't help but notice the pinboards devoted entirely to future weddings, created by young women. In fact, my daughter-in-law leads a weekly Bible study of sixth grade girls and shared that some of the girls in her group have dream wedding pinboards.

The pinboards are filled with everything from engagement settings and wedding dresses to the floral bouquets and monogrammed burlap bags that hold the guest favors. When their Prince Charming finally does arrive, they might want to hold off on showing him the dream wedding pinboard until, oh say, after he proposes! One glimpse at the 1½ carat, princess-cut solitaire engagement ring on the pinboard and the poor lad may hop on his white horse and giddyup on outta town. Sites like Pinterest are feeding into young women's deepest desires to live happily-ever-after . . . one dream wedding at a time.

Someday, My Prince Will Come

The chick flicks and fairy tales subscribe to a familiar formula. The titles may vary, but they all contain the same key ingredients: a perfect prince; a perfectly adorable princess (whose life is drab and incomplete without a man); and a resulting pursuit, or as I like to call it, a "rescue mission." This is the part where the perfect prince comes to the rescue of his maiden in distress and promises to make her life complete. (Translation: He will spend the remainder of his days devoted to adoring her every waking moment of his day. And of course, dreaming about her at night.) He seals the deal with a kiss and voilà . . . happily-ever-after officially begins.

And we eat it all up. Why else would be pay nearly $10 (double that if you want a soda and popcorn) to sit through a two-hour story that has been engineered to prey on our emotional näiveté. Somewhere, deep within our souls, we want to believe that fairy tales do come true. *Sweet Home Alabama, Notting Hill, When Harry Met Sally, The Notebook, You've Got Mail, The Proposal,* and most of the other cathartic tearjerkers spend the bulk of the plot on the moments leading up to the altar.

By the time the credits roll, we've bought the lie (again) and exit the theater wishing our husbands/boyfriends/princes-we've-yet-to-meet would take a few cues from Prince Charming, Jerry McGuire, Troy Bolton, Edward Cullen, or the fabulous Mr. Darcy (from my personal favorite, *Pride and Prejudice*) and get this perfect prince thing figured out. Just once, I would love for my husband to cup my face in his hands and utter Mr. Darcy's heart-stopping line: "You have bewitched me body and soul. And I love—I love—I love you." Is that too much to ask?! I don't even think the man has ever uttered the word "bewitched" in his entire lifetime. "Witch" maybe, but I digress. Chances are, you can not only list your favorite chick flicks on command but also recite verbatim a few favorite romantic scenes, as well.

Here are a few swoon-worthy lines that may be on your list of favorites:

Rhett Butler: "You should be kissed, and often, and by someone who knows how." (*Gone with the Wind*)

Harry: "I came here tonight because when you realize you want to spend the rest of your life with somebody, you want the rest of your life to start as soon as possible." (*When Harry Met Sally*)

Anna: "I'm also just a girl standing in front of a boy asking him to love her." (*Notting Hill*)

Noah: "The best love is the kind that awakens the soul and makes us reach for more; that plants a fire in our hearts and brings peace to our minds. That's what you've given me and that's what I hope to give to you forever." (*The Notebook*)

Frances: "I'm scared of walking out of this room and never feeling the rest of my whole life the way I feel when I'm with you." (*Dirty Dancing*)

Westley: "Death cannot stop true love. All it can do is delay it for a while." (*Princess Bride*)

Mr. Darcy: "My real purpose was to see you, and to judge, if I could, whether I might ever hope to make you love me." (*Pride and Prejudice*)

Dorothy: "Shut up, just shut up. You had me at 'hello.'" (*Jerry McGuire*)

George: "You want the moon? Just say the word, and I'll throw a lasso around it and pull it down. Hey, that's a pretty good idea. I'll give you the moon." (*It's a Wonderful Life*)

Melanie: "What do you want to be married to me for, anyhow?"
Jake: "So I can kiss you anytime I want." (*Sweet Home Alabama*)

Joe: "Don't cry, Shopgirl. Don't cry."
Kathleen: "I wanted it to be you. I wanted it to be you so badly." (*You've Got Mail*)

Rick: "If that plane leaves the ground and you're not with him, you'll regret it. Maybe not today, and maybe not tomorrow, but soon, and for the rest of your life." (*Casablanca*)

Rose: "I'll never let go, Jack. I promise." (*Titanic*)

If you didn't dab your eyes at least once, you are not human. In addition to the movies, we have a slew of reality shows devoted entirely to the process of choosing the bride or groom (*The Bachelor* or *The Bachelorette*), planning a wedding (*Whose Wedding Is It Anyway?*, *Bridezilla*) and purchasing the perfect wedding gown (*Say Yes to the Dress*). Like the movies, they highlight the sprint to the altar but ignore the marathon that follows. The fairy tale always ends before the marriage begins. No wonder so few girls are prepared for the realities of marriage or for the Prince Charming letdown that is sure to follow. Our culture has made an idol out of the wedding day and a mockery out of marriage.

We've been indoctrinated since birth that "someday, our prince will come." And when he does, we want him to sweep in Jerry-McGuire style and declare that we complete him. Bonus points if he interrupts our book club meeting and makes the declaration in front of a living room filled with our best girl-friends. More bonus points if he looks like Tom Cruise. The chick flicks give us a brief two hours to see love through the lens of how it should be—or at least how we *think* it should be. Imagine the disappointment for women who, in the aftermath of their romance binge, encounter a husband who is laid out on the sofa, more mesmerized with the football game on the TV than their cute selves. Or a boyfriend who would rather focus on his fantasy football team than take them out for frozen yogurt and tell them how wonderful they are . . . again, for the third time this week.

My oldest son, Ryan, has jokingly dubbed the chick flicks as "emotional porn," arguing they are as dangerous to women as porn is to men by creating unrealistic expectations about the opposite sex. The quest for Mr. Right has been replaced with the quest for Mr. Perfect; and, alas, no guy on this earth can measure up to the impossible chick flick standard. Pastor and author Tim Keller says, "We maintain the fantasy that if we find our one true soul mate, everything wrong with us will be healed. No lover, no human being, is qualified for that role. No one can live up to that. The inevitable result is bitter disillusionment."[1] Regardless of the truth, women, both young and old, continue to buy the lie that a man will make them happy.

Prince Not-So-Charming

When I met my husband, Keith, I was a mess of a girl with a mess of a past. I actually met him on the same day I became a Christian at a retreat for college students. I guess you could say

I met my Prince Charming and my one true Prince on the same day. In my first few months as a new believer, Keith played a vital role in helping me plug into a local church and encouraged me to join a small-group Bible study. I had never really read the Bible, so I would often call him with questions about passages that were difficult to understand. I was amazed by his knowledge of the Bible and spiritual maturity. I remember telling my roommate, "Whoever marries Keith Courtney is one lucky girl." Never did I imagine that I would be that girl. When we began dating, I was completely and totally smitten. To say I had put him on a pedestal would be an understatement.

Once we were married, it didn't take long for him to fall off that pedestal. Or maybe I knocked him off. Funny how some of the "qualities" we once found cute or endearing about our spouses during the dating or engagement phase can become downright annoying in marriage. For example, one of the character qualities that attracted me to my husband was his frugality. It brought me security to know he was committed to setting aside money for retirement. Once we were married, I quickly realized that we had two completely different ideas of what constituted "frugal." Try convincing a lawyer of the necessity of owning multiple pairs of black shoes and see how far you get. My brilliant arguments about closed-toe versus open-toe versus wedges versus stilettos were lost on the man. He just mumbled something about our kids (the ones we had yet to conceive) not being able to go to college someday because of their mother's affection for black shoes. At least I'd look good when I dropped them off at the campus student loan office!

If I had a nickel for every time he uttered, "It's not in the budget" in the early years of our marriage, I'd have all the money I need to support my black shoe habit. "The budget" this . . . "the budget" that . . . yada, yada, yada. What began as an annoyance eventually morphed into bitterness and anger when I began to compare my husband to other husbands who didn't seem to be as concerned with the budget. If I've learned anything at all about the comparison game, it's that you'll walk away a loser every time because you will always compare another man's good qualities with your husband's faults. It's not a fair comparison. Once we begin to pick out the best qualities in other men and add them to our long list of expectations for our own husbands, we're in trouble. We are at high risk of having our hearts being swept up in an idealization of what the perfect soul mate might look like. There is an added danger when we fool ourselves into believing another man might be a better match for what we think we "need." The mere thought that such a man exists can take root in our hearts and produce untold amounts of damage if we're not careful. There is no such thing as the "whole package" when it comes to a husband or a wife. Every person comes with flaws, so let's be careful not to cherry-pick the best qualities we see in other men and create a mental prototype of our perfect soul mate. We certainly wouldn't want our husbands doing the same when it comes to other women. It's ironic how when I would complain to one of my close girlfriends about my husband's annoying frugal habits, they often would express frustration over their husband's tendency to be a spendthrift. While I was busy comparing my husband to their husbands, they were busy comparing their husbands to my husband.

I'm picking on my husband's habit of frugality, but trust me when I say that I had my own long list of annoying habits that I brought into our marriage. Add to the equation that we had our children early into our marriage, and as a result my husband's needs often went unmet. Unfortunately neither my husband nor I had the tools we needed to get down to the root of the problem and process our frustrations. We buried them and let them fester for years. To further complicate matters, I expected that a good Prince Charming would be able to read between the lines of every heavy sigh, eye roll, door slam, and tear to follow.

Like many couples, my husband and I hit a wall in our marriage that eventually landed us in a counselor's office around the eight-year mark. As I look back today with twenty-five years of marriage under my belt, I realize that much of what landed us in counseling could be traced back to unrealistic expectations we each brought into marriage. In a nutshell, I had somehow imagined that my long-awaited prince (a.k.a. soul mate) would be able to anticipate my needs, wants, and desires without having to ask and subsequently meet those needs. (Translation: Read my mind.) My husband, on the other hand, expected me to speak up and let him know what I was feeling and what I needed. (Translation: Communicate with him.)

In counseling, we learned to fight fair. We learned that stuffing our emotions and allowing bitterness to take root is as unhealthy as a screaming match and cross words. In addition, we learned how to communicate more effectively when it came to sharing our hurts and daily frustrations. My husband, like many men, tends to jump immediately into problem-solving mode rather than empathize with how I might be feeling. On top of that, he has an engineering background, which means his solutions to the problem will be accompanied with flow-charts and graphs to better illustrate his point. Oh, I kid, but it has certainly felt like that at times. The problem was, I didn't want solutions. I simply wanted empathy. If I shared about my chaotic day juggling the kids' activities and my home-based business, he would offer up a buffet of possible solutions to better maximize my time. What I really wanted to hear was, "I'm sorry you had a rough day. How can I help reduce your stress?" Boom, all done. There is a time to offer solutions, but in my mind it comes after empathy has been offered.

On the other hand, I learned that it takes my husband awhile longer to process decisions. Just sending him to the store for toothpaste can cause him to lapse into a full-blown episode of paralysis of analysis when he sees all the choices on the shelf. Bless his engineering heart. Mint flavored, tartar control, whitening, sensitivity, fluoride—it's just too much for him to process. I can knock out the entire shopping list before he finally commits to a tube of toothpaste. He thinks everything through before making a decision. Unfortunately, he's married to little-miss-fly-by-the-seat-of-her-pants, who sometimes forgets to think things through. Like the time when I was leaving our church's Vacation Bible School and someone was giving away free kittens in the parking lot. (Note: If you don't want a kitten, then don't allow your children to "take a peek" into the box of free kittens. Walk away. Don't look back. Burn rubber out of the parking lot, but get out of there!) One look at that little furry face staring back at me and the next thing I know, I'm a cat owner. It happened just like that. I should mention that we don't even *like* cats.

Had I involved my husband in that very important decision, he might have worked up a spreadsheet detailing the pros and cons of cat ownership. He probably would have thought through such details as it needing to be fed on a regular basis or that it would require a litter box that needed to be cleaned out regularly. He might have even noted the possibility that one of us (me) would be allergic to the cat. In the "cons" column, he might have mentioned the cat's ability to shed its body weight in cat hair and the end result that family members would wear the cat to school and the workplace daily. And I'm sure he would have listed the biggest "con" of all in cat ownership: That small, teeny-tiny detail that our family doesn't even *like* cats. Kittens, yes. But not cats.

Even knowing my husband needs time to process decisions, I still have a tendency to act on my emotions and expect my husband to hop on board. This is probably something I should remind myself more often . . . so perhaps I would know better than to drop a bombshell at the dinner table just months after becoming emptynesters that it would be a good idea to look into fostering/adopting older children from the state's foster care system. I probably should have thought through the timing of that one a bit more before making my emotions-based announcement. Even after twenty-five years of marriage, my husband and I are still learning to communicate in a way that honors each other.

The Princess and the Plea

We all walk into marriage with a mental list of expectations. When those expectations go unmet, we feel let down. Whether your husband fails to fulfill a request on your honey-do list, forgets to pay the cable bill on time, doesn't spend enough time with the children, fails to read your mind that you could use a little help in the kitchen, or puts on an extra thirty pounds since your wedding day, it is only a matter of time before he lets you down in some form or fashion. And then there are the letdowns of a more serious nature. A husband who is distant and aloof. Or forgets a wedding anniversary. Or looks at porn. Or has an affair. No one walks into marriage expecting to be disappointed at that level, yet many of you have that testimony.

While in the course of writing this very chapter, I met a precious pastor's wife at an event where I was speaking. She shared with me that just weeks prior, she had discovered her husband was having an affair. In spite of her letdown, she voluntarily stood up at the end of the event and, through tears, uttered one of the most profound lines I will ever hear in my lifetime. She said, "Over the past week and a half, God has reminded me that he cares more about my heart and the heart of my husband than my personal happiness."

I don't know many Christians who could say that, in the immediate aftermath of such a painful betrayal. Most of us would have taken to the bed for weeks—after, of course, tossing our husband's belongings out on the front lawn. My new friend and her husband have a long road of healing before them, but I have a hunch they are going to be OK. Regardless of the outcome, my friend will rise up from the ashes of this firestorm with an impenetrable faith because she has put her hope in the only Prince who could truly satisfy her heart. He will not fail her. God cares more about the refining process and our hearts than our personal happiness. Do you believe that?

It's time to let our husbands off the hook when it comes to completing us. They are not qualified for the part. They are as broken and in need of restoration as we are. Proverbs 19:22 sheds light on our deepest need: "What a man desires is unfailing love" (NIV). God wired our hearts to crave love, but the part of the Prince has been miscast. Try as they may, our husbands cannot love us perfectly. Nor can we love them perfectly. There is only one perfect Prince who can deliver perfect, unfailing love, and that's Jesus Christ. There is no greater love story than the story of God's redemption. While we were still sinners, Christ died for us. There is not a chick flick that can match the Romans 5:8 rescue mission: Jesus, suffering a brutal death on the cross to pay the ultimate price for our freedom, knowing we would still sin. It just doesn't get any better than that. Ladies, our Prince has already come. Put him on the pedestal of your heart and let your husband off the hook.

True love has nothing to do with romance and everything to do with redemption. ❦

Notes

1. Timothy Keller, *Counterfeit Gods* (New York: Penguin Group, 2009), 29.

Chapter 3

P-31 Flunkie

My first brush with the Proverbs 31 woman occurred during my junior year of college. I was attending a weekly Bible study, and our group leader gave us the charge to read the Proverbs 31 passage so we could discuss "what it looked like to be a Proverbs 31 woman" the following week. The other girls in my group let out a collective sigh, which in hindsight should have been my first clue. "The Proverbs 31 *who?*" I asked. The leader seemed a bit shocked over my apparent lack of knowledge regarding this particular Bible character. She kindly explained that this was the gal to emulate when it comes to the pursuit to become a godly wife and mother. I was not raised in a Christian home, so I welcomed any guidance I could get in my new Christian walk and looked forward to reading the passage.

Later that evening, I opened my Bible to Proverb 31 and began reading the passage, beginning in verse 10.

> A wife of noble character who can find? She is worth
> far more than rubies. (NIV)

Off to a good start. I mean, how hard could this Proverbs 31 stuff be? I would soon find out. I continued reading . . . and reading . . . and reading. By the time I got to the verse where she makes her own bed coverings, I wanted to curl up in my own store-bought comforter and sleep off my depression. Was this woman for real? No wonder she's worth far more than rubies. She's doing the job of twenty people. If there was ever a poster child for adult ADHD, this is the gal. Did she stay hyped-up on a steady string of 5-hour Energy drinks to knock out her daily to-do list? The woman cooked, cleaned, sewed, ran a business, invested in real estate, tended to the poor, and could still "laugh at the days to come" (Prov. 31:25 NIV). Well, good for her. If this was the template for becoming a godly wife and mother, I was in big trouble.

I wondered if the passage was supposed to be interpreted literally. At the very least, I would need to learn to cook. And sew my own clothes. And cut coupons. And buy a glue gun.

If there's a verse in there about scrapbooking, I'm toast. Count me out. So, I did what any other reasonable woman would do after reading the passage for the first time. I closed my Bible and made a vow never to read the passage again. Oh, I kid. But not really.

By the time my weekly Bible study rolled around, I had compiled a long list of questions to ask my leader. I was intrigued by the verses that described this woman's entrepreneurial spirit and keen business sense. Working outside the home didn't seem to match up to the modern-day church-lady mentality I had been exposed to in my short Christian walk. Unfortunately, we never really got around to unpacking the verses about her work outside of the home. My leader and the rest of the girls in the group seemed content to camp on her domestic to-do list in our attempt to crack the code of what it looked like to be a modern-day Proverbs 31 woman. In the end, we were left with a June Cleaver-like prototype of domestic Leave-It-to-Beaver suburban blissdom. Being the impressionable new Christian in the group, I didn't question the conclusion and resigned myself to the fact that becoming a godly wife and mother would require that I learn how to make flaky biscuits from scratch and sew the family bed coverings. The "smiling" part would come later, I figured, when the hubs and kids fulfilled their role to "rise up and call me blessed."

Married to the Beau

One year later, I was engaged to be married, and lo and behold if June Clever wasn't my future mother-in-law. She made things from scratch. She knew what a colander was and how to use a garlic press. She could make a bed and get an A+ on the military quarter-toss test. She cut coupons out of the newspaper and actually used them. She was rather intimidating to say the least. My culinary skills were limited to Kraft Macaroni & Cheese and frozen corn dogs. Laundry was not my forté, given that I grew up with two working parents and a housekeeper who managed the household chores. I had no idea how to operate a washer and dryer until my freshman year of college when I finally ran out of clean clothes and was forced to give it a try. On my first attempt, I ended up shrinking an expensive angora sweater I had borrowed from a friend. Who knew some things are supposed to "lay flat to dry"?! When the sweater emerged, it was a perfect fit for my current four-pound Yorkie. I handed my friend a wad of cash and vowed to take my dirty clothes home for the holidays when I would sneak them into the washroom before the maid arrived. I had a lot of catching up to do before the big wedding day.

Needless to say, my husband and I encountered a few domestic hiccups in that first year of marriage. My husband was a real trooper when I tossed his underwear and undershirts into the washer with a pair of never-been-washed-before red sweatpants. Pink may be all the rage for men today, but it most certainly was not chic in the 1980s. But no doubt, the lowest moment came when I overheard my husband on the phone one evening asking my mother-in-law (a.k.a. June Cleaver) how to "get the mildew smell out of towels." Oh boy. That conversation definitely came up in a marriage counseling session down the road. I may or may not have threatened to strangle him with one of those mildewed towels if he pulled that stunt again. Just dry off, Bud, and spritz yourself with some Febreze. Problem solved.

If I made any improvements in that first year, everything proceeded to go downhill when the kids arrived on the scene. I tried to pull off the domestic image of a home-cooked meal simmering on the stove top when my husband walked through the door, but more often than not, I was the one boiling. Blame it on the stress of cooking in an extremely hostile work environment—also known as I-have-three-young-children-who-melt-down-at-the-dinner-hour. After a day filled with wiping little bottoms, sweeping up Cheerio-strewn floors, and debating with toddlers about their favorite drink cup being in the dishwasher, the predinner hour was often my tipping point. Maybe I missed the scene in the show where June locked Wally and Beav in a closet while she prepared her signature dish of fake stove-top stew, but I couldn't seem to juggle the roles of mom, homework advisor, chef, and lover all in the same night. And let's not forget, our friend June also had time left over to touch up her makeup, change into her Sunday dress and pearls, and reshellac her Aqua Net hair helmet as part of the preprimp ritual before Ward's grand entrance. Sorry, but if you know someone who's pulling that off on top of the home-cooked meal, chances are that mom has a full-time chef, nanny, and maid. And should my husband dare to follow Ward's example and make a beeline for the La-Z-Boy recliner right after he walks through the door, he won't be getting any dessert later that night, if you know what I mean.

During those crazy, chaotic preschool years, I reread the passage and discovered a verse I had overlooked before: "She is like the merchant ships, bringing her food from afar" (Prov. 31:14 NIV). Folks, if we needed biblical justification for picking up takeout, I think we just found it. I didn't resort to restaurant food every night, mind you. Just some nights. Look at it this way—some families have "taco night," and the Courtney family just happened to have "taco week." My family is living proof that you can survive a steady diet of tacos, spaghetti, frozen skillet dinners, and supermarket rotisserie chickens and be just fine. Just pray your kids don't rat you out for your lack of experience in the kitchen.

One of my dear friends recently reminded me of a time when my youngest was in kindergarten and came over to her house for an after-school play date. She fired up the toaster oven and served up a batch of Tyson frozen chicken nuggets. Hayden devoured the meal and said, "Mrs. McEntire, that meal was delicious. Can you please give my mother the recipe?" Pathetic. Don't worry; she was faithful to give me the recipe, so I added those to my shopping list, as well.

Sock It to Me

My Proverbs 31 breaking point came at a women's conference I attended many years ago. The theme was, you guessed
it, "The Virtuous Woman." I remember being loaded down with
guilt as the main speaker defined what qualities constitute a
modern-day virtuous woman, touting Proverbs 31 as the foun-
dational passage for her inside knowledge. I can't recall many
of the details, but I do recall that she spent a good five minutes
highlighting the importance of wives sorting their husband's
dress socks by color in their dresser drawers. I am not making
this up. I skimmed the passage to find that verse but with no
luck. (Maybe it was included in the King James Version: "Thou
sorteth her husband's socketh drawer.") Apparently, sock sorting fell under the umbrella of bringing her husband "good, not
harm, all the days of her life" (Prov. 31:12 NIV).

My laundry insecurities reemerged, and I felt sufficiently
browbeaten as the speaker blabbered on about loving our
husbands enough to separate their blue, brown, and black
socks in labeled plastic bins contained within the sock drawer.
If I'm remembering correctly, she may have even given us a
demonstration with actual props, but I could be wrong. She
even exhorted us to put the brown socks in the middle, since
blue and black socks are often mistaken for one another. If this
unknown sock clause is a deal breaker for attaining Proverbs
31 status, I had no choice but to resign on the spot. What
next? Was she going to tell us to give up our Altoids for those

awful-tasting Testamints in the quest to become "virtuous"?! I'm sure there's probably a verse for that attribute too.

When I got home from the conference (and let me just remind you that this really is a true story), I held it together pretty well. Until, that is, I made my way into the master bedroom, where I was met with a tall plastic laundry basket of socks. Some were still in the basket, but others had cascaded to the floor surrounding the basket. Up until the conference, this sock system had worked just fine in my home. Clean laundry made its way into my bedroom and was dumped on the floor to be separated out and delivered to the appropriate rooms. Folding was optional. Socks were corralled and placed into the tall plastic laundry basket otherwise known as Grand Central Sock Station. Mama Courtney doesn't sort socks, pair socks, mend socks, label socks, or bleach socks. Socks were a nuisance, and therefore, they all lived together in perfect harmony in the plastic laundry basket. When someone needed a pair of socks, they just went into my bedroom and rifled through the basket until they found two that worked. A matching pair was optional and not likely. On this particular day, the basket literally looked like it had thrown up socks all over the floor.

Seeing this sight directly following the sock-sorting seminar—uh, I mean the virtuous woman seminar—I tumbled over the Proverbs 31 edge. I took one look at my Mount Everest sock pile and burst into tears. My husband (who I might add was wearing a pair of matching socks, thank you very much) rushed to my side to see what had brought on the sudden tears. I pointed to the sock pile and through tears said, "I'm a terrible wife. I want to be one of those Proverbs 31 women who cooks homemade meals every night and cleans the baseboards, and organizes your sock drawer by color, but I just can't do it all." He looked thoroughly confused. I went on to tell him about the speaker's advice to "do our husbands good by arranging their socks by color." To which he replied, "Huh?" Then he began to laugh and said, "I don't know who this lady is, but if you're going to 'do your husband good,' most men would prefer their wives care more about their lingerie drawer than some stupid sock drawer." So there you have it.

Maybe some women have time to organize their husbands' sock drawers in addition to everything else on their home management list, but I'm not one of them. I know my limits and I also know what's more important to my husband, which is why after twenty-five years of marriage, he is more than happy to keep digging through the sock basket at the end of our bed each morning (while I sleep soundly, I might add). I'm sure there have been plenty of mornings where he showed up to work wearing (gasp!) one blue sock and one black sock, but trust me, he's a happy, happy man. Now, sock lady's husband . . . I'm not so sure. But bless his heart, he's never lacking in the sock department.

P-31 Myth Busters

At least one good thing came out of the sock seminar. It motivated me to dive into the Proverbs 31 passage and study it on my own, rather than rely on other people's preconceived notions of what constitutes a modern-day Proverbs 31 woman. In fact, it led me to write a Bible study called *The Virtuous Woman*. In the process of writing the study and researching many Bible commentaries, I made a startling discovery: The Proverbs 31 was not an actual, real woman. All these years I'd felt intimidated by this woman, only to discover she's make-believe! Santa Claus, the Tooth Fairy, the Easter Bunny, and the Proverbs 31 woman—all in the same category. Only this chick doesn't leave gifts behind, except for maybe a big dose of guilt. The passage is actually a compilation of virtuous qualities that women should strive to have. Whew. We are off the hook.

Theologians speculate the verses were written by either Lemuel, Lemuel's mother, Solomon, or possibly some unknown person. It's possible that Lemuel is the poetic name for King Solomon, but no one really knows. While we can't be certain of the identity of the king referenced, we can conclude that the passage was a reflection of a mother's teaching to her son. The first lead-in verse of the Proverbs 31 passage states, "The words of King Lemuel. An oracle that his mother taught him" (ESV). The next eight verses relate to the dangers of "strong drink" (drunkenness) or giving your "strength to women" (adultery). The final twenty-two verses in the passage relate specifically to a description of an "excellent wife," or as some translations note, a "virtuous woman" (a.k.a. The Proverbs 31 woman).

Once I began to unpack the Proverbs 31 passage, it became evident that the stereotype of the Proverbs 31 woman is not only lacking but also inaccurate. The passage does not describe a mild-mannered church lady whose primary purpose is to be a housekeeper and helpmate to her spouse. I'm certainly not knocking those qualities, but we've gotten way off track with portrayals that limit her to this role only. One Bible commentary notes, " . . . the noble wife of this chapter supervised a staff of workers (v. 27). She served as buyer for her enterprises (v. 13). She sold what her staff produced (vv. 18–24), and she invested her profits (v. 16). She had the freedom to give to help the needy (v. 20). She was respected for her wisdom and responsibility (vv. 14–15, 26–31)."[1] Each of these is a "business" function, and while the woman's activities were linked to her home and family, the biblical picture of the woman's role is a far from only the "stay-home-and-care-for-the-kids" model.

Why are these qualities rarely addressed when we hear about the Proverbs 31 woman? This is no Bible-totin' June Cleaver, friends. In fact, the Hebrew word for "noble" in verse 10 is *chayil* (khah´-yil), which means "a force, whether of men, means or other resources; an army, wealth, virtue, valor, strength; band of men (soldiers), company, host, might, power, riches, strength, strong."[2] This woman was a force to be reckoned with and it was this brand of virtue that made her a rare find with, "worth far more than rubies" (v. 10 NIV). Whether or not she works full-time, part-time, or is a stay-at-home mother is irrelevant as long as she is fiercely devoted to her God, her husband, and her children—in that order.

The Crowning Virtue

At the core of the virtuous woman's devotion is her relationship with the Lord. It trumps every other quality on the list. "Charm is deceptive, and beauty is fleeting; but a woman who fears the LORD is to be praised" (Prov. 31:30 NIV). The virtuous woman serves her family because she first serves God. She is strong for the task because she draws her strength from God. She ministers to the poor out of an overflow of what God gives her. She is efficient because she views her work as a divine calling rather than a job. She can laugh at the days to come because she finds her joy in the Lord (and knows that the future belongs to him anyway!).

This woman is no weak-willed doormat, so be careful about believing stereotypes that may portray her in that fashion. They don't tell the whole story. She is a mighty force who is vigilant in her devotion to God and family. That devotion is packaged in many different types of women. She may be the woman at your church who makes a mean seven-layer dip for the church potluck or the woman in your Bible study group with multiple tattoos and piercings. She may be the woman who works full-time or the woman who stays home with her children. She may be the woman who is divorced and tackles her single-mom duties with a smile on her face, but a burden in her heart. She may be the woman who bakes her bread from scratch, or the woman who picks up pizza twice in the same week. She may be the woman whose house is as clean as a whistle or the woman who hires someone to clean for her. She may be the woman whose husband plucked his socks out of a color-coded sock drawer after eating a delicious home-cooked breakfast before he headed out the door for work. She could even be the woman whose husband heads out the door for work in the morning sporting a pink undershirt under his pinpoint oxford and a blue and black dress sock under his suit trousers. After, of course, he polishes off a plate of Eggo frozen waffles toasted to a golden crisp by none other than . . . himself. Theoretically speaking, of course. ~~🍃

Notes

1. L. O. Richards, *The Bible Readers Companion* (Wheaton: Victor Books, 1991), 394, electronic edition.

2. J. Strong, S.T.D., LL.D. *A Concise Dictionary of the Words in the Greek Testament and The Hebrew Bible* (Bellingham, WA: Logos Research Systems, Inc., 2009).

Chapter 4

Save the Date

I love receiving "save-the-date" engagement cards in the mail and seeing the creative ideas that go into some of the photo shoots. One of my favorites was a collage of pictures of the soon-to-be-wed couple. One photo featured the couple playing a board game on a blanket in the park, mouths agape with laughter; another of them showed them swinging side by side on a swing set while they looked at each other with a flirtatious sideward glance; and yet another shot was taken behind as they walked hand in hand toward a beautiful sunset.

While the pictures were breathtaking, I have to also admit they tapped my inner cynic. Would this happy couple in the pictures still be playing board games in the park ten years from now? Swinging on the swings at the park? Walking hand-in-hand into beautiful sunsets? Or would this couple, like so many others, look back at their engagement pictures years later and wonder where their fun friend in the pictures went?

I know this pattern all too well. With great anticipation, I walked down an aisle and married my best friend on May 23, 1987. Within four months, we discovered we were expecting our first child. Our one-year anniversary was spent at a Lamaze childbirth class. In hindsight, we would have been better off going out for a romantic candlelit dinner, since I chucked all the breathing techniques on delivery day and resorted to screaming "epidural!" until I got my way. Exactly thirteen months after our wedding day, our son was born.

By the time the labor and delivery nurse could finish saying, "It's a boy!" our identities as Mr. and Mrs. had shifted to Mom and Dad. Two more children followed, and before we knew it, date nights, snuggling on the sofa, and passionate embraces were replaced with late nights, colicky infants, and clingy toddlers. We told ourselves that someday, when the children weren't so dependent on us, we'd have time to focus on being a couple again. But someday never arrived. There was only so much time in a day and most of it was devoted to the children. We didn't mean for it to happen. It just did.

By our five-year anniversary, we had a five-year-old, a three-year-old, and a newborn. Our lives revolved around our children and their never-ending needs. Add to the equation early labor and bed rest with two of the pregnancies and an infant that was labeled as "high need" by the pediatrician. This basically translates into "she didn't sleep through the night for one year and was only happy when attached to my hip or breast." If that weren't enough, my youngest child required surgery at five weeks for a blockage to the stomach.

When I look at the happy couples staring back at me on the save-the-date cards, it causes me to flash back to the difficulties that come with juggling marriage and parenthood. I know how easy it is to lose the friendship, romance, and intimacy when the children arrive on the scene. As I mentioned earlier, this led to my husband and I sitting in a Christian counselor's office just short of our eighth anniversary with a marriage on life support. We both wanted to be that happy couple in our engagement and wedding photos, but we didn't know how to get there again. Even in the midst of the noise and chaos of three young children, we both felt desperately alone. We each wanted our friend back.

By far, one of the best takeaways we learned during our counseling sessions was the importance of scheduling regular, consistent date nights. Date nights had been one of the first things to go when we became new parents. Aside from the fact that it was costly to get a babysitter and go out to dinner, it was impossible to get out the door without the kids melting down in the background. Year after year, we made excuses. Without a designated date night that gave us time to focus on our relationship without interruption, the kids became our common bond. They were the topic of 99 percent of our conversations. Our counselor pointed out that one of the greatest gifts you can give your children is to show them what a healthy and happy marriage looks like. Pass down to them the legacy of a godly marriage. At the counselor's request, my husband and I agreed to start "dating" again to rebuild the friendship. Without a friendship as the foundation, true intimacy—the kind God intended for marriage—would not be possible.

Today, my husband and I are experiencing the benefits from making an investment in our marriage in the earlier years. This past year Keith and I celebrated our twenty-fifth wedding anniversary. The year before, we married off two of our children, dropped our youngest child off to college for his freshman year, and became grandparents. Talk about a year for celebration! As we sat across from each other one evening at a restaurant that overlooked the jewel-toned beaches of Jamaica, we marveled that it didn't seem like twenty-five years of marriage had passed. At one point, I looked across the table and was overcome with emotion at how very much I loved the man sitting across from me. With tears in my eyes, I reached across the table, grabbed my husband's hand, and told him, "Thank you for being committed to dating me all these years."

I honestly believe our commitment to prioritize a date night at the eight-year mark saved our marriage. We didn't insist on a date night once a week, but very rarely would two weeks go by without a date. And we didn't always force our-selves to have heavy conversations about our relationship. We used our date nights to coordinate our calendars and make sure we were on the same page when it came to parenting our children. Sometimes, we used our date nights to work through difficulties that came up in our marriage. We had learned the hard way that unresolved conflicts would eventually produce a root of bitterness if not addressed in a timely manner.

By far, the biggest benefit was the valuable time spent together as a couple. We realized how much we had missed each other when we began going on weekly dates. We started cutting up and laughing again and having fun. We acted like a married couple rather than two roommates who happened to live in the same house and parent the same children. In the process of dating, we became better parents, and we modeled what a healthy marriage looks like to our children. Our chil-dren knew that our relationship with each other was a higher priority to us than our relationship with them. When we dropped our last child off at college and we officially entered the empty-nest chapter of life, my husband and I didn't have to endure the awkwardness of reacquainting ourselves with each other. We already knew each other from our countless date nights over the years. We just picked up where we last left off . . . and increased the number of date nights!

It's not a coincidence that the divorce rate for couples over fifty has doubled in the last twenty years.[1] Many empty nesters are nothing more than roommates by the time their last child leaves the nest. If you have tied the bulk of your identity into your children and their various activities, you are setting yourself up for a world of hurt when the last child leaves the nest. And as a recent empty nester, let me assure you: that day is coming. I can't think of anything lonelier than losing your children on one day and then waking up next day to a virtual stranger each and every morning thereafter. Your best investment is to make your marriage a priority before your children leave, so you have your very best friend by your side to celebrate the empty-nest chapters of life. And trust me, it is a celebration!

Date nights don't have to be defined by expensive dinners and a night away from the kids. They don't even have to take place at night. "Date nights" are simply a block of designated time devoted to the marriage rather than the children. In fact, I asked some fellow mothers with children to weigh in on Facebook with their own budget-friendly date-night ideas. Regardless of your schedule or income level, there is something for everyone.

Creative Date-Night Ideas

We have what we call "downstairs date night." The kids stay upstairs after dinner. My husband and I make popcorn and watch a movie on Netflix or from Redbox. ~Anne, married 9 years

We enjoy trying new foods so we eat at different places each month. You can search coupons for restaurants online. On occasion, to save money, we trade watching kids with another couple. We get our girls, ages eight and seven, involved by allowing them to pick out our clothes for the date. They have been known to offer other fashion tips along the way. {grin} ~Tobi, married 20 years

We try to have a date night once every couple of weeks. Most of the time our date nights consist of a nice dinner, but occasionally we enjoy doing free art walks in our local arts district or take our camera on a local "road trip" and snap pictures of things that catch our eye/inspire us. In between date nights, we try to spend time together after our children go to bed as well; it usually consists of watching a couple of episodes of our favorite television show. ~Brandi, married 17 years

We have a standing weekly date—Saturday morning breakfasts. Every single Saturday my husband gets up and makes ME breakfast! As we eat together, we talk and get all caught up on each other's week and dream about the future together. Our breakfasts often last two hours (or more) as we sit together just chatting and sipping coffee. It truly is my favorite "date." ~Robin, married 29 years

We have six kids ranging in ages from four to sixteen, so much of our time revolves around their daily activities. We usually get away by ourselves about once a week to go out to eat and watch a movie. Sometimes in the evenings, we walk around our neighborhood for thirty minutes, which is a great time for us to talk without being constantly interrupted. We do our best to spend quality time with each other alone each day even if it is only for five minutes to discuss the day's events! Last weekend we enjoyed our alone time by picking out plants for our yard at a local nursery. It is sometimes the little moments such as these that are surprisingly fun and meaningful. ~Robyn, married 20 years

Friday nights have always been our night. Occasionally we go all out, but most often we just keep it simple and inexpensive (or free). We also try to get away once or twice a year for at least a night or two. It is so important to make time for family, but more importantly to make time for each other. It's also important to show our boys that making time for each other is a priority. It nurtures security and confidence. ~Carla, married 21 years

I make sure the kids have plenty of activity during the day, so both go down for bed by 7:30. We go out back, watch the stars and talk, or sip on some wine and listen to music by the fire. There's no cost, just a lot of preparation during the day so I can have kiddos down early for us to enjoy our evenings. This way we still put ourselves first daily, and "date nights out" are an extra bonus. :) We do have three date nights per month on average. ~Jen, married 8 years

Seriously, I know that sounds silly, but we love going to Costco or Target together without our kids. Sometimes we go out to dinner if we can afford it. ~Carly, married 13 years

We have a scheduled date night once a month but rarely leave the house. I make the kids dinner and get the little kids to bed and the big kids interested in something in another part of the house while my husband and I have dinner together and typically watch a movie. Sometimes we light candles, and sometimes we order takeout. We talk and laugh and just relax, but we are together without interruption. One of the best date nights we have had this year was when my husband drove me to the next county over, and we went to see the very first house we ever lived in. We stopped by old "stomping grounds" and were amazed at how things had changed. We drove home in a lightning storm that was like beautiful fireworks closing our evening. Sometimes it's the little stuff that makes for the most fun. ~Brandi, married 18 years

Our favorite is sitting under the stars. Very cheap. Very romantic. ~Dannah, married 23 years

My husband is in ministry and off on Fridays. We have our date time while the kids are at school. Sometimes we go back to sleep when they leave. We'll go to a movie or if on a budget that week, get a free rental from the library. Lunch ranges from a nice restaurant to a picnic on the living room floor. ~Theresa, married 20 years

We try to go out at least once a week. Sometimes it is just for coffee or a drive in the country. It helps us reconnect like when we were dating! ~Dori, married 20 years

Ideally, it would be good to have a designated date night weekly or bimonthly. In addition, I highly recommend that you get away for a long weekend at least once a year. If you don't have family in town to watch your children overnight, consider swapping with another family you trust. And keep in mind that if the budget doesn't allow for a hotel, you could always stay home while the kids spend the weekend with friends or family. In addition, start saving toward a bigger trip where you can get away for a longer period of time. I know it's hard to fit it all in, but what better investment than the future health of your marriage? If you have slacked off on having regular date nights, let me encourage you to stop right now and approach/call/text/e-mail your husband and ask him out on a date. Spend the first date talking about your weekend getaway trip or dreaming about where you can go for a bigger trip.

One Is the Loneliest Number

In Genesis 2:18, God said, "It is not good for the man to be alone. I will make a helper suitable for him" (NIV). Mind you, Adam was living in paradise and had a relationship with God, yet God determined he needed a companion. God intended marriage to minister to our aloneness. However, it's possible to be married for many years and feel desperately alone. The key to reducing our loneliness in marriage is to nurture a deep and intimate friendship with our husbands—apart from our children. The only way to accomplish this is to make time for the friendship. Share common interests together. Flirt with each other. Laugh together. Share your dreams. Hold hands. Hug often. Be goofy. Send each other texts throughout the day. Plan getaways. Take up a hobby together. Don't put it off any longer. We make time for the things we deem to be important.

Many Christian families have bought into the lie that the needs, wants, and desires of the children should come before the needs, wants, and desires of the parents. Kid-centric homes have become the norm in our culture, and as a result, the marriage relationship has been put on a back burner in many homes. In fact, one woman who answered my question about creative date night ideas said, "If we go on a date night, it is rare. Maybe twice a year. But we do have family night a few times a week, which is like a family date." This is a dangerous line of thinking that many Christian couples have adopted. Family date nights do not prioritize the marriage—they prioritize the children. Of course, there is nothing wrong with having family date nights as long as you have carved out time for your marriage first. Take it from this empty nester: those kids are going to leave you someday. I know it's hard to imagine that day will come when you are right smack in the daily grind of parenting. The truth is, you will spend the majority of your years with your husband, not your children. You need time alone with your husband away from your kids. Children who grow up seeing their parents prioritize the marriage are more secure and confident in the long run.

In his book *The Meaning of Marriage*, Tim Keller writes that God "didn't put a parent and a child in the Garden," but "a husband and a wife. When you marry your spouse, that must supersede all other relationships, even the parental relationship. Your spouse and your marriage must be the number one priority in your life."[2] Keller goes on to say that the purpose of marriage is for "helping each other to become our future glory-selves, the new creations that God will eventually make us." He states, "that is why putting a Christian friendship at the heart of a marriage relationship can lift it to a level that no other vision for marriage approaches."[3]

I realize that some or you are reading this and your marriages have lapsed beyond friendship into the roommate phase. Maybe it seems awkward and uncomfortable to talk to your husband about having a regular date night. I encourage you to broach the topic, even though it may be met with resistance. If you have not made the marriage a priority, admit your mistake and ask for forgiveness. It may be necessary for some couples to get some extra help from a professional Christian counselor, just as my husband and I did. It was one of the best investments (both in time and money) we've ever made.

My husband and I were out on a date on a recent evening at one of our favorite hole-in-the-wall cafes, best known for its chicken fried steak, fried okra, and coconut cream pie that's more meringue than pie. The café is located in a retirement community and, therefore, caters to a large senior citizen crowd. In fact, nearby assisted-living residences will load up their buses and make this café a regular outing. My husband and I always joke that we feel so young when we eat at this café. I love to observe people and couldn't help but notice an elderly couple that sat in a booth and never once looked up at each other or exchanged a single word. It was as if they had run out of things to say, long ago. I can't imagine the pain of living out the remainder of your years in silence. In a sense, they were already widowed.

And then there was another couple that I noticed when a hostess seated them at a table nearby. The husband pushed a walker in front of him and shuffled so slowly with the tiniest of steps that I wondered if they'd make it to the table before closing time. The wife was not the least bit flustered with him and stood by his side with her hand cupping his elbow and matched his pace, inch by inch. While he focused on the task at hand, she wore a sweet smile as she spoke tender words of encouragement to him along the way. Every so often, he would glance up to the side and give her the sweetest smile. I desperately wanted to go sit with them and ask them their secret to such a happy and healthy relationship. Had I done so, I wonder if they would have offered that they never, ever stopped dating. What a contrast to the other couple sitting a few tables over in silence. I know which couple I want to be, but it won't come without commitment and hard work.

Save the date . . . and save the marriage.

Notes

1. Greg Clary and Athena Jones, "Baby Boomer Divorce Rate Doubles" (June 24, 2012), *CNN Living*, http://articles.cnn.com/2012-06-24/living/living_baby-boomer-divorce_1_divorce-rates-baby-boomers-first-marriages?_s=PM:LIVING.

2. Timothy Keller, *The Meaning of Marriage* (New York: Penguin Group, 2011), 119.

3. Ibid., 112.

Chapter 5

Unmet Sexpectations

On my long list of questions to ask God when I get to heaven is: "What's up with the different sex drives between men and women?" In the book *Making Sense of the Men in Your Life*, author Kevin Leman says, "Men reportedly think about sex an average of thirty-three times per day, or twice an hour. Some people say women think about sex only once a day—when men ask for it."[1] When my husband and I were in the thick of the exhausting baby and toddler years, sex quickly got bumped to the bottom of my to-do list. Notice I said "my" and not "our." Yeah, it was still at the top of hub's list. Call me a slow learner, but in twenty-five years of marriage I have learned something about the basic needs of men. In case you're wondering, here they are (in no particular order):

1. Sex.
2. More sex.
3. Have I mentioned, a whole lotta sex?

OK, they need food too, so go ahead and put that at #4. It wasn't until later in my marriage that I realized how important sex is to men. In fact, that epiphany occurred while I was writing a chapter on sex and the boy brain for my book, *5 Conversations You Must Have with Your Son*. Most of the background research I did compared an adolescent boy's drive for sex to a hunger that never quite goes away. And then it hit me. The same is true for men. The hunger is always there.

> Imagine how difficult it must be for our husbands to live in a world that is all too happy to take advantage of their sexual hunger pangs—around the clock. Author Rick Johnson adds: At the risk of perpetuating a stereotype about men, there's a distinct possibility that if women knew how and what men really think about, they would refuse to be in the same room with them . . . They'd think them perverted. Guys think about sex all the time. Men even think about sex in the most inappropriate places, such as in church or at funerals. The slightest and most

innocent thing—a woman's laugh, the curve of a shapely leg, certain shoes, perfume, and thousands of other scents, sights, and sounds—can set men off.[2]

As women, we have a tendency to discount our husband's sex drive as over-the-top, rather than view it as a result of how God wired them. And this is where it gets complicated. The more stress factors women add to our plate (translation: kids, long workdays, kids, sleepless nights, kids, financial pressures, kids, body image issues, etc.), the less we want sex. Whereas, the same stress factors don't diminish our husband's desire for sex in the least. In fact, some might argue men want it even more as a means to relieve the stress! In other words, the desire for sexual intimacy stays at the top of their list, while it simultaneously gets bumped down further and further on our lists. And we all know where that leads—to a never-ending debate about how much sex is enough.

Elle Magazine and MSNBC.com conducted a reader survey over a two-week period of time during which they asked 77,895 readers, half women and half men, about their sex lives. When asked the question, "How often do you have sex?" most men and women said they have sex once or twice a week. Yet, when they examined the answers based on gender, men think they're having sex less often than women. Men said they have sex a median of 5.5 times a month while women said 8.4 times.[3] Generally speaking, women overestimate the frequency of sexual intimacy while men underestimate it. Surprise, surprise. When was the last time your husband made a move for sex and you thought (or said out loud), "Honey, we just did it the other day!" If you said it out loud, your husband likely responded with a lightning-quick Rain Man calculation down to the exact number of days, hours, and minutes since your last sexual encounter. More important, he's counting the days until he can have sex again. If there's a countdown app for that, our husbands probably have it as a screen saver on their phones.

Hunger Pains

A man's continual focus on sex reminds me of a new "old-people" habit my husband and I have developed as recent empty nesters. While on a dinner date, we found ourselves talking about where we wanted to eat the following night—before our food had arrived. Our kids make fun of us for things like this, but hey, if that's our biggest worry in the empty-nest years, I'll take it. I imagine this is what it's like for many husbands when it comes to sex. Before they wrap up one encounter, they are dreaming about the next one. On the other hand, we are thinking, *Whew, that should hold him off for a few days.* Now, stop for a minute and think about how devastated they feel when an entire week goes by . . . or two weeks . . . or more between sexual encounters. It is a hunger, much like the hunger we might have to make an emotional connection with our spouses on a steady basis. Let me stop here for a minute and say that there are some men who don't meet this description and seem to have a lower libido than is typical and some women have a higher libido than is typical. Ultimately, the point remains that getting on the same page in the bedroom necessitates understanding each other's desires and coming up with a compromise.

In the course of writing this chapter, my daughter-in-law was over one afternoon and we were talking about how my grandson is in a particularly cranky stage and was regressing back to waking up in the middle of the night. She couldn't quite figure out what the problem was. He wasn't cutting teeth or running a fever, so it was a mystery. A few days later, she called to tell me that she had figured out what had been making him so fussy: he was going through a growth spurt and wasn't being fed enough! She checked the pediatric charts related to how much formula and baby food he should be consuming on average per day, and he was under the average for his age. The poor kid was starving, and, of course, my daughter-in-law was overcome with mother's guilt. (Get ready, sweetie, there's more of where that came from!) Never mind that the boy has roly-poly thighs and little baby ankles.

Most mothers would react exactly as my daughter-in-law did: initial horror upon the discovery that the baby was hungry, followed quickly by massive amounts of guilt. The solution, of course, was to provide more food to address the baby's hunger. We as mothers wouldn't stop until we figured out exactly how much food our child needed to address his hunger. Certainly, none of us (I would hope) would respond with an attitude of "Ugh. I fed you yesterday. Get over it!" I think you know where I'm going with this. Why then, would we treat our "hungry" husbands any differently? Now granted, our husbands aren't going to die if they don't have sex, but you get my point. Our husbands are supposed to be a greater priority to us than our children, so shouldn't we care if they are starving sexually or at the very least, need a little more to satisfy their hunger? Our husbands are completely dependent on us to meet their sexual needs (if they are honoring God's plan), which puts us in a pretty powerful position of control.

Think of something that is extremely enjoyable to you. Maybe you enjoy the adrenaline rush you get from exercising a certain number of days per week. (OK, maybe not.) Or perhaps a weekend girls' getaway trip you take each year means the world to you. Or, for the mothers of little ones, maybe it's just a simple Sunday afternoon nap. For others, it may be a fiction book you enjoy reading in your downtime or a favorite TV show you watch regularly. Now, imagine if you thought you were going to be able to do that special something and then you didn't get to after all. A week goes by. And another week. And yet, another. It would be even more disappointing if that something remained just within your reach but was constantly withheld. Now imagine if the almighty gatekeeper that stands between you and the something you were anticipating was your husband. Bitterness would likely set in, with resentment close behind, nipping at its heels.

According to the survey I mentioned above, one in five marriages is considered to be "nonsexual," meaning the couple engages in sex fewer than ten times a year.[4] If you find your-self in this category, I urge you to broach the topic with your spouse and take a next step in figuring out why your marriage is "nonsexual." Many factors can cause a low libido in both men and women. Whether it's due to medical issues, a hor-mone imbalance, or a multitude of deep-seated hurts that have occurred within your marriage, these issues can be treated with some professional help. It may be uncomfortable to broach the topic, but the survival of your marriage may depend on it.

Equal Rights in the Bedroom

In 1 Corinthians 7:3–5, Paul advised:

> The husband should fulfill his wife's sexual needs, and the wife should fulfill her husband's needs. The wife gives authority over her body to her husband, and the husband gives authority over his body to his wife. Do not deprive each other of sexual relations, unless you both agree to refrain from sexual inti-macy for a limited time so you can give yourselves more completely to prayer. Afterward, you should come together again so that Satan won't be able to tempt you because of your lack of self-control." (NLT)

I want to tackle the last part of the passage above first because it gives the "why" behind Paul's advice for husbands and wives to meet one another's sexual needs.

In verse 5, he clearly stated that the deprival of sex can lead to a lack of self-control on the part of the deprived spouse, which can make him or her easy prey to temptation. Barry McCarthy, a Washington, D.C., psychologist and sex therapist, says, "When one or both partners are dissatisfied with their sex lives, it plays an enormously negative role in a marriage, and is a top reason couples get divorced. Those couples who treat sexuality with benign neglect often stumble into a crisis, whether it's a man using porn or the woman falling in love with someone else."[5] One survey found that 48 percent of men who cheated on their wives did so because they wanted more sex and 47 percent did so because they wanted more sexual variety.[6] It certainly doesn't excuse the betrayal and sin, but given 1 Corinthians 7:5, we can't ignore it as a factor that leads to temptation toward sin.

One Bible commentary had this to say:

> Paul stressed the equality and reciprocity of the husband and wife's sexual relationship by emphasizing the responsibilities of each to satisfy the other. Some in Corinth were trying to practice celibacy within marriage. Apparently this refraining from sex within marriage was a unilateral decision of one partner, not a mutually agreed-on decision (vv. 3–4). Such a practice sometimes led to immorality on the part of the other mate.[7]

Unfortunately, the practice of one partner withholding sex from the other seems to be all too common. Maybe you can relate but would argue that you are not making a conscious decision to withhold sex from your partner. Sex just doesn't happen, like folding the clothes or remembering to turn on the dishwasher before you leave the kitchen. Whether your reason for withholding sex is passive-aggressive or just old-fashioned neglect, it is not an innocuous action. The person depriving the other partner of sex is in total control. He or she is in the driver's seat.

Scripture advises married couples to agree on how to meet each other's sexual needs. For example, if your husband prefers to have sex every other night (above the average norm), but you're good with once every two weeks (below the average norm), a compromise would be to aim for twice a week. Both of you are compromising in an effort to meet in the middle. By establishing an expectation about the frequency of sex, disappointment (and possibly its stepsister resentment) are less likely to occur.

More than a Number

I don't want this to sound like a simple math equation. The sexual relationship between a husband and wife isn't that simple because no relationship can be evaluated by numbers. However, I do believe it's wise for couples to talk openly about their expectations about sex. If you have no idea how many times per week your husband would prefer to have sex (guessing or assuming doesn't count), I want to issue you a challenge. Set aside some alone time with your husband (nonsexual) and ask him this bold question: "Realistically speaking, about how many times a week would you like to have sex?" The purpose behind the question is to better understand your husband's sexual appetite and expectations. If you truly care about the health of your marriage, you will ask the question. And if your husband is a God-fearing man who also cares about the health of the marriage, he won't take advantage of the situation by replying with an unreasonable answer (seven nights a week, fifty-two weeks out of the year!).

Every couple develops its own formula for a healthy balance regarding sexual needs. What is reasonable for you and your husband may not be reasonable for your best friend and her husband, so resist the urge to compare your situation to others' (also known as "ammunition"). Determine what works best for you and your husband—as a couple. And remember, needs change. What may be reasonable one year may not work if you have an infant in the house. Revisit this topic on occasion to ensure you are both on the same page.

Refusing to talk about sexual needs and appetites can be a silent killer to a marriage. Very rarely will a husband be completely open with his wife when his sexual needs are not being met. Very few will take the initiative to say, "Honey, I fear if my sexual needs are not met and this becomes an ongoing pattern, I may cave into the temptation to resort to porn or have an affair." He may be afraid of rejection, an ensuing argument, or that you'll think poorly of him. Unmet sexual needs most often simmer beneath the surface and produce an untold amount of collateral damage on down the road.

Sex is a critical component in a healthy marriage for both men and women. Unintentional neglect is still neglect. At some point down the road, there will be a price will become apparent. I learned a hard lesson about the price of neglect when I was in my last year of college. A few years prior, my parents had given me a brand-new Ford Mustang. Unfortunately, I did not follow the guidelines of suggested car maintenance by having the oil and antifreeze levels checked on a regular basis. My approach to car maintenance was, "If it ain't broke, don't fix it." Unfortunately, that approach cost me a good bit of money when my hood began to emit black, acrid smoke one day while on a road trip. My engine gave out on the overpass of a busy freeway and my car had to be towed to a garage. The antifreeze had completely run dry and as a result, my engine block had cracked. That one little crack in the engine would cost several thousand dollars to repair.

The car was nearly new. It looked perfectly fine on the outside. Yet, under the hood, hidden from plain view, signs of neglect were evident. The end result could have been prevented had I only maintained the car along the way. The same is true for our marriages. Sex is a regular part of marital maintenance that impacts the long-term health and endurance of the marriage. Is your marriage overdue for a tune-up?

Five Ways Couples Can Get on the Same Page with Their Sexpectations

1. Determine how often (on average) per week each partner desires sexual intimacy and come up with a compromise.

2. If you're struggling to find time to be intimate, consider determining in advance which nights would be best each week, so there are no surprises. With advance notice, you can work together to put the kids down earlier, fix supper earlier, or finish projects more quickly in an effort to give each other priority. Of course, exercise grace when necessary. This is only a guideline, not a rule that can't be broken.

3. Try not to put off sex twice (or more) in a row. This can lead to the other partner feeling frustrated and fearful a new pattern might be emerging. Of course, extenuating circumstances occur (this is life!), but a make-up night goes a long way if you have to skip.

4. Learn the art of the quickie. While it's ideal to take your time with sex, some nights just don't lend themselves to that. Agree in advance that either partner can call a "quickie night." (Just don't get in the habit of making every night a "quickie night.")

5. Talk with your spouse about what you each feel comfortable doing or trying in the bedroom (or outside the bedroom!). If you're too embarrassed to broach the topic, send your husband a text or e-mail and ask him what

he would enjoy. This will get the conversation started. If you are mutually comfortable with something, give it a whirl. Sex is a gift to be enjoyed. God never intended shame to be a part of the equation. ～☙

Notes

1. Kevin Leman, *Making Sense of the Men in Your Life* (Nashville: Thomas Nelson, 2000), 130.

2. Rick Johnson, *The Man Whisperer: Speaking Your Man's Language to Bring Out His Best* (Grand Rapids: Revell, 2008), 134.

3. See http://www.msnbc.msn.com/id/12410076/ns/health-sexual_health/t/what-you-said-when-we-asked-about-sex/#.T-EvV_GHdFo, "What you said when we asked about sex; All the juicy details of the Elle/MSNBC.com reader survey," msnbc.com; updated May 9, 2006.

4. Ibid.

5. See http://articles.chicagotribune.com/2010-12-15/health/sc-health-1215-how-often-sex-20101215_1_unmarried-couples-relationship-sexual-problems; Barry McCarthy, a Washington, D.C., psychologist and sex therapist, and coauthor of the new book *Enduring Desire*.

6. Alex Elejalde-Ruiz, "Sex and the Married Couple: Keeping It Fresh and Frequent Feeds Intimacy and the Relationship" (December 15, 2010), *Chicago Tribune.*

7. J. F. Walvoord, R. B. Zuck, and Dallas Theological Seminary, *The Bible Knowledge Commentary: An Exposition of the Scriptures* (Wheaton, IL: Victor Books, 1983), 1 Corinthians 7:3–4.

Chapter 6

Duty or Desire?

In the previous chapter, we examined how married men commonly view sex. In summary, it's at the top of the list for most men. In this chapter, I want to take a closer look at common attitudes about sex among married women. I realize two back-to-back chapters on sex may seem like overload, but I feel strongly that this is an issue we cannot ignore if we are to make our marriages a priority. I purposely led with the Save the Date chapter as it is important to first build a foundation of friendship and trust in your marriage that will, in turn, have a direct impact on other important components of the marriage, such as a healthy sex life. Couples who are committed to building a friendship in marriage are less likely to feel uncomfortable talking about their sex lives. Dating produces intimacy and playfulness, and that will overflow into the bedroom. If you are missing the friendship component in your marriage as well as struggling with issues related to sex, turn your attention to building the friendship first. It will do wonders for your sex life.

I recall a girls' get-together where the topic of sex came up. The conversation went something like this, "Ugh, honestly, I could take it or leave it." And another gal chimed in, "If I could lose this extra weight, I would probably like it again. My husband said it doesn't matter to him, but it matters to me." And yet another shared, "I just don't understand why they want it so much! Get over it!" All of the women who were present are in committed Christian marriages. We all love our husbands very much. Some have been married in the single digits; others for much longer. But around the circle that night, we were all unable to understand our husbands' appetites for sex. Better yet, we all struggled to adapt to their appetites and match desire with desire. We all admitted to times when sex felt more like a duty or a chore than a passionate pursuit.

When my kids were young and extremely needy, sex became a mere afterthought in my marriage. My unspoken logic amounted to: "Hey, there's only so much of me that can go around. Sorry, hubs, but you're the only one in this bunch who stands over two feet and can fend for yourself, so get in line—behind the infant in need of a diaper change, the toddler with the unexplained rash, and the kindergartner who's responsible for selling thirty pounds of cookie dough for the T-ball team by tomorrow's practice." On many days, I counted the hours until the kids' bedtime. My husband was counting too, but for a different reason. Finally, I would arrive at that magical moment when I would collapse into the bed, thankful to have survived yet another day, only to glance over at my husband and be met with the look. You know the look I'm talking about. The "I need you" look. And I would usually give him a look back that says, "Touch me and prepare to die." I'm betting you can relate. Most of us are just too distracted, exhausted, emotionally spent, and completely drained to make sexual intimacy a priority.

Apparently, we are not alone. The sex survey conducted by *Elle* magazine and MSNBC.com sheds some light on the most common reasons men and women cited for not having sex on any given night. The survey asked the question, "What are some reasons why you didn't have sex in the last month?" Among women, 42 percent said they were too busy or stressed, 34 percent cited different bedtimes than their partner, 35 percent said they weren't interested, and 23 percent said feelings about their body made them less interested. With men, 53 percent said their partner wasn't interested, 47 percent said they themselves were too busy or stressed, and 38 percent cited different bedtimes.[1] Note that men reported the top reason for not having sex was a partner's lack of interest. Also note that men did not cite lack of interest on their part as a reason. Again, we see the contrast in sexual appetites between women and men.

God's Design

God created sex to be more than a means to populate the earth. He also created sex for our enjoyment in marriage. Most importantly, He intended sex to be the glue that bonds husband and wife together in a trusting, loving relationship. Genesis 2:24 says, "A man will leave his father and mother and be united to his wife, and they will become one flesh." In the course of writing the book *5 Conversations You Must Have with Your Daughter*, I stumbled upon some fascinating scientific research that supports this biblical principle of "two becoming one." Neuroscientists have discovered a hormone called oxytocin that is released during sexual activity. This same hormone triggers contractions and induces labor and signals the release of breast milk after the baby is born. Oxytocin is known as the "bonding hormone." It bonds mother and child—and husband and wife. In addition to bonding, oxytocin has also been shown to increases trust. Makes sense, doesn't it? A baby develops trust in the mother who will provide and nurture and protect. A husband and wife develop trust in each other to protect and to support and to encourage. Always and forever. Until death do you part.

God intended marriage to be a physical, emotional, and spiritual experience, something much greater than the current culture's notion of a purely self-centered pursuit. God intended sexual intimacy to bond the husband and wife together and to build trust between them. Without sex, the husband and wife can become nothing more than roommates who wear matching wedding bands and play house. For this reason, we must work to overcome the hindrances that commonly contribute to our waning desire for sexual intimacy.

"I'm Too Tired!"

I imagine that most of you reading this can relate to the most common reason given for a lack of intimacy: too busy or too stressed. Few would argue that stress and busyness go hand-in-hand, and few could argue that both are as common in our daily lives as cooking dinner or paying the bills. If we can solve the busyness problem, we will be left with less stress and more time to enjoy other things—like sex. Sex is one of many areas that can get lost in a sea of overcommitments and frazzled living.

Women need more time to warm up to sex, so we need to allow for plenty of time in the evening to wind down and relax. I know this may sound unrealistic to many of you, especially if your children are young and desperately dependent on you. *Relax* is not a word in your vocabulary. However, we often create stress in our lives by saying "yes" too much. Take an inventory of your day to see what you could potentially release as a responsibility. Do you really need to do Project A? Are you really the only one who can coordinate day care? We're going to tackle busyness in a future chapter, since it's a problem that plagues most of our lives; but given the impact it has on intimacy, I want to encourage you to begin thinking about how to create time to relax in your schedule.

Also examine the factors that contribute to increased stress in the evening. Do you need more help with the kids' homework or bedtime routines? I bet your husband would gladly take over many of the evening duties if he were to understand that those duties have a direct link to your level of sexual desire. One friend's husband takes over dinner and bedtime duties on the nights they are planning to have sex. A couple of nights a week they have "grill night," since her husband is more familiar with throwing things on the grill than whipping up something on the stove. My friend likes the arrangement so much that she recently told me she is considering upping the "grill nights" per week!

When my husband and I were in the early years of our marriage, we agreed on a similar arrangement. I basically informed him that there would be cookin' in one room of this house: the kitchen or the bedroom. I let him pick. Needless to say, my children have been raised on a steady diet of takeout, Kid's Cuisine meals, and DiGiorno frozen pizzas. They can share that information with their counselor someday, after, of course, they process the trauma of having their childhood photos handed to them in Ziploc bags rather than Creative Memories scrapbooks. (For the record, I also apologized to the youngest child for receiving far fewer Ziploc bags. I had to confess to him that I wasn't even quite sure if the pictures were of him, since I had long since given up writing names and dates on the back of the pictures. I told him to feel free to get with his brother and sister and sort out who was who.)

Dinnertime was often the tipping point in my day that could set the tone for the rest of the evening. Maybe it's something else for you. Are there items on your to-do list that could be delegated? Simplified? Omitted? Put off for another night? At the end of the day, we are the ultimate masters of our calendars. We make time for the things we deem to be important, and if sex isn't currently on the (top of the) list, it may be time to redefine our priorities. When we fail to make sex a priority, we send a message to our husbands that other things are of greater importance to us. Keep that in mind as you take an inventory of your day. Oftentimes, we go overboard in an effort to be the best mom possible to our children, and in the process we neglect our husbands' needs. I've certainly been guilty of that. The truth is, many of us are more focused on creating a pleasant bedtime routine for our children than we are for our husbands.

I found it interesting that one of the most common reasons both women and men gave for not having sex in the survey I mentioned above was "different bedtimes." When I was a young wife and mother, a mentor of mine encouraged me to resist slipping into the habit of going to bed at a different time than my husband. After seeing the survey results, I can certainly see the wisdom behind her counsel. For the most part I have heeded her advice, and at times I have worked late into the night tapping away on my laptop while my husband sleeps beside me. He is used to it and has said he would rather have me next to him when I'm working late than off by myself in another room of the house. If different bedtimes are an issue in your marriage, consider coming up with a plan where both you and your husband go to bed at the same time on a majority of nights per week. Even if sex is not the goal in mind, being together at the end of the day builds intimacy. For couples whose work schedules may prevent them from going to bed at the same time, it will be necessary to find a "good" time to have sex.

"I Hate My Body"

Another common reason for not wanting to have sex is body image issues. If this is a factor for you, consider talking openly with your husband about your insecurities. Don't expect him to read your mind and know this is the issue. Chances are, he has assumed your disinterest has something to do with him, and he feels rejected. My prayer is that he will reassure you of your desirability and offer empathy. I'm a big believer in exercise, not just as a means to look good but also as an outlet to feel good. The better we feel about our bodies, the less inhibited we will feel in the bedroom. Of course, this will require a willingness to reorder our priorities to free up some time to exercise. Even walking around the neighborhood will do wonders for improving our body image.

We may also need to readjust our attitudes when it comes to our postpregnancy bodies. Few women return to their previous prepregnancy weight and shape, so let's stop this nonsense of tying our body image to the bathroom scale. Embrace your new curves; and while you're at it, allow your husband to embrace them too! If you have some extra weight to lose, commit to eat better and exercise more, but don't punish your husband in the interim. We'll tackle body image issues in a future chapter, since this issue has produced so much fallout for women—fallout that eventually trickles down into our marriages.

I want to pause here and say that if you find yourself stuck in an ongoing pattern of not wanting to have sex, you may want to consider seeing a professional counselor. You could have a medical issue or a hormone imbalance that is perpetuating the lack of drive. Or perhaps, the issue is unresolved bitterness toward your spouse for a hurt that occurred earlier in your marriage. Perhaps a childhood trauma still affects you in a negative way. Regardless, please consider taking the first step to discover the root of the problem. If your marriage is a "low-sex marriage," don't ignore the problem and assume your husband is on board with little to no sex. Most men silently starve and grow more and more bitter as the days and months tick by. Acknowledge the problem, even if you have to go to your husband and say, "I know we have a problem, and I want you to know that I'm committed to doing something about it, but I need your help and support." Yes, it takes guts to face the problem, but what do you have to lose? A few awkward minutes to broach the topic could change the quality of your marriage.

Duty or Desire: Does It Matter?

Leaving our husbands with the impression that we are having sex out of duty rather than desire can have a negative influence on our spouses' self-esteem and confidence. In her book *For Women Only*, researcher Shaunti Feldhahn reports that 97 percent of men say they want to feel desired and sought out by their wives, not simply tolerated when they want to have sex.[2] Sighing heavily or rolling your eyes when he initiates a move, lying there like an unresponsive robot, glancing at the clock, and comments to the effect of "Didn't we just do it the other night?" can severely damage their fragile esteems. Most men take great joy in pleasing their wives. A handful of men are selfish lovers and if this represents your marriage, I'm very sorry and I encourage you to consider counseling or meet with someone at your church to address the problem.

Psychologist and sex therapist Barry McCarthy advises, "The challenge for couples is to integrate a sense of intimacy—closeness, warmth and predictability—with a sense

of eroticism, which is about playfulness, creativity and taking sexual risks. While every couple is different, as a general
guideline, couples should aim for non-demand pleasuring four
to seven times a week (such as touching, cuddling, foot rubs)
and intercourse one to three times a week."[3] Broaching the
topic can be difficult, but ignoring it can kill a relationship.

Sex is a beautiful gift from God to married couples. He
intended it not only for child-bearing purposes but also for our
pleasure. In Song of Solomon (or Song of Songs, depending on
your Bible translation), sex is clearly described as a means of
pleasure. One Bible commentary says,

> The Song of Songs is a beautiful picture of God's
> "endorsement" of physical love between husband and
> wife. Marriage is to be a monogamous, permanent,
> self-giving unit, in which the spouses are intensely
> devoted and committed to each other, and take delight
> in each other. . . . The Song of Songs shows that sex
> in marriage is not "dirty." In fact, in Song of Solomon
> 7:11–13, the "beloved" or Solomon's wife takes the ini-
> tiative by requesting sex from her husband.[4]

Enjoy sexual intimacy and do away with the guilty hang-
ups. Initiate sex on occasion. Speak up and tell your husband
what you like, and ask him what he enjoys. If married couples
can't talk about these things, who can? Anything is fair game
within marriage as long as both partners are willing and
the act does not cross a biblical line (for example, viewing

pornography). Marriages with a deep level of physical intimacy are less likely to encounter problems related to pornography, lust, or adultery on down the road.

I want to make a couple of disclaimers that I feel are important to address. I realize this chapter may be a difficult chapter
for some to read. I don't want to minimize the pain that can
result from unmet sexpectations. Unfortunately, a small minor-
ity of men may have an inaccurate view of biblical submission,
which could translate into some warped ideas about what sex
should look like in marriage. This saddens me a great deal.
Please know that I am in no way suggesting that wives submit
to unwanted sexual advances from their husbands or agree to
do things they are not comfortable doing. The thought sickens
me. In fact, if you are in such a marriage, please seek professional help at once. Sex is not about taking but, rather, mutual
giving.

I also want to acknowledge that some women may lack a
desire for sex due to a past history that includes sexual abuse.
I that is your situation, I am very sorry for your pain. Make it
your goal to be open with your spouse about your past in order
that you are not alone in your suffering. If necessary, schedule
an appointment with a licensed, professional Christian counselor to help you take the next step in your recovery.

Unfortunately we can't talk about intimacy in marriage
without talking about the problem of men viewing porn, many
of whom do so on a regular basis. I am in no way pointing the
finger of blame at the wives. Nor do I have any tolerance for a

position that implies it may be their fault. Everyone is responsible for his or her own choices and actions. Many men carry a habit of viewing pornography into their marriages, and it does an untold amount of collateral damage—physically, emotionally, and, especially, spiritually. If you are married to someone struggling with pornography, I am so very sorry. I know this chapter and the one preceding it must be very difficult to read and process in light of the fact that your husband's habit and sinful choice will have a direct impact on your sex life. Again, if this is your situation, I implore you to do something. Anything. But speak up and bring the issue out of the darkness and into the light. Insist on counseling and employ tough love if need be. Make it your goal to take a forward step of progress. Any step. Just take one.

Five Ways to "Desire" Your Husband

1. Send your husband a calendar request for a "play date." (Just make sure calendar requests don't go through his secretary first!)
2. Ditch the fuzzy house shoes, flannel pants, and granny panties. It only takes a minute to change into something sexy, and it will send a message to your husband that he is a priority.
3. Send him a daring text during the day and tell him: "I know you've been stressed lately. Tonight's all about you." Include a picture, if you dare.*

4. Find a sitter and plan a quick weekend getaway. Take the initiative and plan to seduce him. Of course, pack your lingerie!

5. Text/e-mail your husband the following day after sex and say something to the effect of, "Wow . . . can't stop thinking about last night. It was awesome."

*Obviously, you need to be very careful if you are going to sext your spouse. Double- and triple-check that you are sending personal pictures or text messages to the correct cell phone number! Make sure your husband's phone is not set to display pictures and texts on the home screen when they arrive. Last of all, delete, delete, delete. ∼☙

Notes

1. See http://www.msnbc.msn.com/id/12410076/ns/health-sexual_health/t/what-you-said-when-we-asked-about-sex/#.T-EvV_GHdFo; "What you said when we asked about sex; All the juicy details of the Elle/MSNBC.com reader survey; msnbc.com," updated May 9, 2006.

2. Shaunti Feldhahn, *For Women Only* (Sisters, OR: Multnomah, 2004).

3. See http://articles.chicagotribune.com/2010-12-15/health/sc-health-1215-how-often-sex-20101215_1_unmarried-couples-relationship-sexual-problems; Barry McCarthy, a Washington, D.C., psychologist and sex therapist, and coauthor of the new book *Enduring Desire* (London: Routledge, 2001).

4. J. F. Walvoord, R. B. Zuck, and Dallas Theological Seminary, *The Bible Knowledge Commentary: An Exposition of the Scriptures* (Wheaton, IL: Victor Books, 1983), Song of Solomon 8:13–14.

Chapter 7

Repeat after Me: NO

Hi. My name is Vicki and I'm a recovering yes-aholic. (Insert soft clapping and head nods by support group here.)

As a young mom, I couldn't say "no" when asked to do something. In the past, this disease has led me to accept jobs I wasn't even good at, like the time I agreed to help coordinate the meals ministry at my local church. Never mind that I don't really cook or that I'm not particularly organized or good at delegation. This basically left me cooking for people I didn't know while my own poor family was starving. I quit after a few months (was fired?) and I have since tried to figure out how to get on the list for a free meal. Twisted ankle, stubbed toe, the sniffles, you name it, and I've submitted our names to the meals ministry in an effort to get my family fed. But they're on to me now.

The problem with yes-aholics is that we are slow learners. We say "yes." We dive into the task. We say "yes" to more things. Then life happens. You know, the unplanned stuff that isn't on our daily calendar, like little Junior forgetting his lunch at his private school twenty miles away, and the Yorkie chewing up a battery someone left on the floor and needing to be rushed to the vet. Of course, all this happens on the same day you signed up to bake five dozen cupcakes for the school's fall festival. Yes-aholics never allow for the unexpected. When the unexpected collides with our already overbooked calendars, it creates a perfect storm for a meltdown.

The problem with saying "yes" to too much is that by default, you essentially say "no" to your family. At the end of the day, your family doesn't particularly care if the things you said "yes" to made the world a better place. You still said "no" to them. But your family members aren't the only ones who suffer. When you say "yes" to too much, you also say "no" to time with God—valuable time you need to refuel and rest. Ecclesiastes 4:6 says, "Better is a handful of quietness than two hands full of toil and a striving after wind" (ESV). I'm pretty sure that over time, I had grabbed up more than two handfuls of toil and it was beginning to show. Once I finally acknowledged I was a yes-aholic, the healing began. Part of the healing process required me to take a deep look at the root of the problem. Why do I have a tendency to say "yes" to too much? Until I could figure that out, the cycle would likely continue.

The Root of the Problem

In Ecclesiastes 4:4, Solomon shed light on a possible reason. He wrote, "And I saw that all labor and all achievement spring from man's envy of his neighbor. This too is meaningless, a chasing after the wind" (NIV). Wait, envy? Isn't saying "yes" typically about helping others? Sometimes. But when we overcommit, our actions are often rooted in our need to be noticed by others. We are a competitive people, and being the best means staying on top of the competition. Like junkies, many yes-aholics hop from one "Atta girl!" to the next, feeling a tiny surge of confidence and self-importance with each compliment doled out. I know. I've been a yes person, and it wasn't pretty. Colossians 3:23a says, "Whatever you do, work heartily, as for the Lord and not for men" (ESV). If I'm in a season of overcommitment, "heartily" is not a word I would use to describe the attitude of my heart while I'm serving. And if I'm honest, I'm not performing as unto the Lord but rather for the applause or attention of others. Coming to this conclusion was painful but necessary.

Another factor that contributed to my overcommitment was allowing others to dictate the "balance" in my life. For example, several years ago my publisher contracted a marketing firm to conduct a media campaign for one of my books for teen girls. The campaign launched during a media frenzy surrounding the abundance of Hollywood girls gone wild. Britney Spears had just shaved her head; Lindsey Lohan had just been busted for cocaine possession; and Paris Hilton had just flashed her nether regions to the paparazzi while she entered a limo. It was the perfect storm for teen girl angst, and moms were scared out of their wits about raising daughters. The marketing firm took advantage of the controversy and pitched me to radio stations to talk about the lack of positive role models for girls. Many took the bait, and I did close to fifty radio interviews in a two-week period. FIFTY. As in, lock me up, people, I've lost my mind. On several of the days, I did six to eight interviews back-to-back. I would literally be wrapping one interview up when the next one would be beeping in on the phone. What in the world was I thinking? And I had other obligations during that two-week period. I had another book deadline, preparation for an out-of-town speaking engagement, carpool duty, and other duties bidding for my attention on the home front. Unfortunately, this is only one of many examples where my failure to say "no" resulted in a tremendous fallout.

My kids needed me. My husband needed me. My staff needed me. My publisher needed my next book. My publicist needed the articles I had committed to write. Publishers awaited endorsements for other authors' books that I had promised to write. I was being pulled at in every direction, and I had nothing left to give. Worst of all, I felt like God was getting the dregs of me. The ministry he had called me to had become a chore. My children's activities had become a nuisance. My husband wanted a wife, not a tired, grumpy roommate. And I wanted my life back.

I hit a wall. I was burned out, bitter, and even angry. I began to blame those who had asked me to do the things I had committed to do. How ridiculous is that?! I'm the one who said "yes." I'm a big girl, and I got myself into the mess. No one was threatening me and forcing me to say "yes." Again, I had to ask myself, "Why couldn't I say 'no'?" In the example of the media campaign, there were several reasons. I felt like I owed it to my publisher to do as many interviews as possible. They had invested a hefty sum into a media campaign, and I wanted them to get the biggest bang for their buck. (As a side-note, my publisher didn't pressure me to do all the interviews and would have intervened sooner had they been aware of the toll it was taking on me.) I wanted the book to do well. I had poured my heart and soul into it, so the competition element was certainly a factor. I sincerely wanted to get it into the hands of as many teen girls as possible because I believed in the message and knew it could make a difference in their lives. So, my overcommitment was partly sincere, partly competitive, and partly due to a sense of obligation. Chances are, you can relate.

Let's examine the reasons a bit more closely because I think introspection is necessary if we are to take a step toward finding a healthy balance. As I dissected my situation with the book interviews, think of a situation in your life when you attempted to rationalize or justify your reasons for your yes-aholic tendencies. When I look back, I can now see that God could prosper my book without a single interview if he wanted to do so. He didn't need a media campaign to accomplish his purpose. He could speak to the hearts of teen girls without the help of my book. Imagine that?! And by acting on a false sense of obligation to my publisher, I shortchanged my family in the end. Why didn't I feel equally as obligated to my family? Could it perhaps have been because they didn't affirm me or sing my praises as much as those outside my house did? Oftentimes, yes-aholics will take for granted the people nearest and dearest to them.

As painful as that season was, it was the wake-up call I needed. I finally learned to say "no." In fact, I went a bit no-crazy at first. I said "no" to radio interviews, requests to write articles, endorse books, and speaking invitations that went beyond my limit of two per month. I blocked off December and the summer months, reserving them for family. I said "no" to requests to help at my kids' school. Little by little, I began to reclaim my life. More importantly, I began to reconnect with God. He reminded me that my worth is only found in him, and rest is a necessary part of the equation when it comes to sitting in his presence. The truth is, God would never endorse a pace (even in ministry) that leaves us so worn out that we have little time and energy for him at the end of the day. On the other hand, I know who would love to keep you busy, frantic, worn-out, beat-up, and used up. Maybe you've heard the saying, "If the devil can't make you bad, he'll make you busy." Satan specializes in luring believers away from their source of life and abundance (John 10:10).

A Much-Needed God-Margin

Psalm 37:7 reminds us, "Be still before the LORD and wait patiently for him" (NIV). The original Greek word for *"still"* is *dâmam* (daw-mam´), which means, "to be astonished, to stop; hold peace, quiet self, wait."[1] Think back at the times in your life when you've been most astonished by God. Chances are, you were giving him your total, undivided, unburned-out attention. I mourn the God moments we miss when we rush through our days, too distracted with the things of the world to sit quietly at His feet. William Penn once said, "In the rush and noise of life, as you have intervals, step home within yourselves and be still. Wait upon God, and feel His good presence; this will carry you evenly through your day's business."[2] Are you running on fumes? Or are you completely out of gas? Matthew 11:28–30 offers the perfect remedy:

> Are you tired? Worn out? Burned out on religion? Come to me. Get away with me and you'll recover your life. I'll show you how to take a real rest. Walk

with me and work with me—watch how I do it. Learn the unforced rhythms of grace. I won't lay anything heavy or ill-fitting on you. Keep company with me and you'll learn to live freely and lightly. (*The Message*)

How are you doing when it comes to "keeping company with him"? If you want to be the best possible wife and mother, you must build a God-margin into your day. Uninterrupted time. Quiet time. Time away from your computer, phone, household chores, noisy children, and the demands of life. Most of us fill up once a week at church, thinking an hour of worship and/or an hour of Bible study are enough to hold us over until the next week. We make the mistake of squeezing God into our busy schedules rather than building our schedules around our time spent with God. Our souls long to be nourished and will not be satisfied with trifle crumbs we grab on the run. Have you built a God-margin into your day? If you read that question and immediately entered into panic mode over the thought that you don't have time left in your day for God, then chances are you are a yes-aholic. Even Jesus took the time to be alone with God. If Jesus needed time alone with the Father, so do we.

Psalm 1:2–3 reminds us that those who delight in the law of the Lord and meditate on it day and night are "like a tree planted by streams of water, which yields its fruit in season and whose leaf does not wither. Whatever he does prospers." Our souls are desperate for spiritual nourishment. Once I began to realize the importance of allowing for a God-margin in my day, I came up with a plan that would work for me.

I try to pick up God's Word in the mornings and read it over coffee. I read through *The One Year Bible* every year, a discipline I began in 2000. I am not always perfectly disciplined, but I pick right back up on the scheduled day when I miss days in between. (Notice I wrote "when" and not "if." Give yourself some grace in your time with God. You won't be perfect!) I also try to read an excerpt out of a devotional book. In addition, I try to reconnect with God later in the day by building a God-margin into my walks. I typically walk three to four days a week and take the opportunity to listen to a sermon podcast from one of my favorite preachers or some of my favorite worship songs on a playlist on my iPod. I cannot begin to tell you of the ways God has spoken His truths into my heart on my walks. Oftentimes, I turn off my iPod and spend the time in prayer. Something about being out in the midst of God's beautiful creation does wonders for my soul. At the same time, it feels good to know I am taking care of God's temple (my body).

I realize that I'm in a different stage of life than you may be. I don't have small children underfoot, so I definitely have a more flexible schedule. The point isn't to do what I do to connect with God but rather for you to build a plan that will work for you. Important elements that you should work on a way to incorporate are some time reading or meditating on God's Word (it could even be one verse!), time for prayer (it could be as you are loading the dishwasher or dryer if that's the only time you have), and to plug into your local church.

Take a minute to think about what might work for you when it comes to building a God-margin into your day. What nourishes your soul? Better yet, how can you get a bigger dose of it? You'd probably be surprised how much time you can find for God just by scaling back our Facebook time. Or cutting back on a favorite TV show. Or, dare I say, limiting our time on Pinterest?

The 12-Step Recovery Plan

Are you a yes-aholic? If so, I came up with a little 12-step program to assist you in the healing process. Consider me a fellow member of your support group and let's head on over to rehab:

The 12-Step Program for Yes-Aholics

1. **Practice makes perfect.** Stand in front of a mirror and say "no." Say it again. Now, say it with a smile on your face and a ring of confidence in your voice. It doesn't matter if it's fake as long as it's convincing. C'mon, do it.

2. **Get a sponsor.** Sometimes it's OK to say "yes," but if you're worried, you may be doing so for the wrong reasons, call a trusted friend or your husband for their perspective. Everyone needs a sponsor (accountability partner) who

understands our weaknesses and can see the situation more objectively.

3. Buy more time. The twenty-four-hour rule is a good rule to have in place when someone asks you to do something. A simple, "Let me pray about it and I'll get back with you" should suffice. This will give you time to pray about it, seek counsel, or make up a really good excuse to tack onto your "no" when the twenty-four hours is up. Oh, I am just kidding. I don't really condone lying, unless of course, the person asking is relentless and continues to badger you for a "yes." In that case, you might try a simple, "My doctor just readjusted my meds and advised me to avoid stressful situations that could trigger another epi-sode." When you say "episode," add a mouth twitch and hand tremor for an added effect. They'll usually back off after that.

4. Politely decline on the spot. If you know you are unable to commit to what is being asked of you, there is no sense in dragging it out. You don't do anyone any favors by hemming and hawing with "maybe's" and "let me check . . . " If you know you can't do it, say "no" and move on down the road. The person asking you is also freed up to move forward and find someone else to do the job.

5. Think beyond the present moment. When you're tempted to say "yes," picture your children ten years from now lying on a black leather couch in a counselor's office and saying: "I don't really remember that much about my mother. When she was on a 'yes' binge, my siblings and I did our best to stay out of her way. I don't even recall what she looked like because her face was always buried in her daily calendar. It was hard being the child of a yes-aholic." Yep, that should do the trick.

6. Quit cold turkey. Prove to yourself that you are capable of saying "no," and abstain from saying "yes" to anything (outside your truly required responsibilities, of course) for a thirty-day period of time. If, at the end of the thirty days, you are not completely satisfied, you can have your "yes" back. Seriously, though. The goal is not to say "no" to anything and everything you are approached to do for the rest of your life, but rather to cut back. Abstaining for a time will help you prove to yourself that you can do it. Look at it as a thirty-day inpatient rehab.

7. Screen your phone calls. Oh wait, did I just say that out loud? I guess I did. In all seriousness, most yes-aholics cave in when they are caught off guard by a smooth-talking recruiter (a.k.a. homeroom mother, church ladies' retreat director, Sunday morning preschool class volunteer coordinator, etc.). If you are trying to recover, you might want to distance yourself from the smooth-talking recruiters until you find yourself in a stronger place.

8. Avoid happy hour. Happy hour to the alcoholic is what Back-to-School Night is to the yes-aholic. Stay away from events like Back-to-School Night where you are likely to be confronted with dozens of volunteer sign-up sheets (uh, drinks) and a chirpy homeroom mom (uh, the bartender) begging for your signature (uh, soul). Call in sick. Skype the teacher later to meet her or him, but whatever you do, don't go into the bar. Oh wait, you say you are the chirpy homeroom mother because you failed to say "no" the year before? Sorry, I can't help you get out of that! Save this list before they ask you to do it again next year. And trust me, they will.

9. Practice a little visualization exercise. If you're tempted to say "yes," fast-forward mentally to the days after the job is done. Now picture yourself in a crisp, white straitjacket being fed applesauce by a mild-mannered nurse in a quiet room with padded walls. Wait, that actually sounds pretty good. Yeah, go ahead and omit this one.

10. Claim the Five kids+ exemption. I'm not sure if you're aware of this, but if you have five or more children who are school-aged or younger, you are exempt from having to sign up for any volunteer activities. This even includes concession stand duty at the Little League fields. The truth is, the rest of us will end up watching your little munchkins on the playground while you serve your time. OK, actually I just made this whole exemption thing up, but really, we all know you're taking life one breath at a time, and a simple request from the team mom for two dozen iced-down Gatorades and trail mix (that the kids aren't going to eat anyway) just may be your tipping point.

11. Reframe your thinking. They say that 15 percent of the people do 90 percent of the work. Maybe it's time we start recruiting the other 85 percent of the people to help us out. Some people don't serve because they lack confidence in themselves and their abilities. If you say "no," consider suggesting someone else who might be a better match for the job. This is different than throwing your friends under the bus and giving out their contact info to the Cutco salesman. (You know, the salesman you couldn't say "no" to and as a result, had to sit through a painful, one-hour sales pitch? Not that you would do that. For the record, I have the nicest cutlery on the block because I couldn't say "no" to that either. I might need to get a second job to pay for it, but it can slice a ding-dang penny in half. Not that I need to slice a penny in half . . .)

12. If you fall off the wagon, don't give up. We all have moments of weakness. If you find yourself lapsing back into your yes-aholic ways, do what you can to reverse the damage. For example, I recently said yes to four back-to-back weekend speaking engagements. Yep, I took a tumble from the wagon. Rather than beat myself up, I vowed to be more careful in the future. The key is catching yourself before you lapse completely back into your old ways.

As with most things, the key is balance. Make your motto, "In all things, moderation." You need to know your limits. Pray about it, and ask God to show you what a healthy balance looks like. The truth is, God doesn't need our acts of service. He wants our hearts. In the next chapter, we're going to talk about how we can better manage the family busyness. Just as we desperately need a God-margin in our day, our family members need one as well. We lead by example, so learning to say "no" on our end is a prerequisite to managing the family busyness. ❧

Chapter 8

Quitting the Family Busyness

I don't remember the exact moment when I entered into the fray of the family busyness, but I do remember the exact moment when I quit. I learned to personally say "no" and began to take back my own life. One taste of simple will leave you wanting for more. But it wasn't enough to reduce my own load. I realized I was still a servant to my kids' never-ending activities.

Somewhere along the way we have bought into the dangerous mind-set that our children should never be bored. Is it possible that we have so carefully orchestrated our kids' calendars and packed them so tight with constant activity that they don't know what to do when there is a rare pause in their day? When many of us were children, our parents didn't have all the options for around-the-clock extracurricular activities. As a result, we got bored. And it was simply wonderful. We would go outside and round up all the other bored kids in the neighborhood and play kickball in the cul-de-sac until we were a sweaty, hot mess. Then we would jump into someone's swimming pool or sprinkler to cool off and play a game of Marco Polo or Hide-and-Seek. In the evenings, we would rush back outside after dinner to play flashlight tag or lie on someone's driveway and look at the stars. I miss boredom. And I didn't want my children to miss the value of being bored.

More important, I wanted my children to know how to slow down and be still before God. To breathe. Relax. They knew how to open their Bibles and say a quick round of bedtime prayers, but they were missing the evidences of God that come throughout the day. It's hard to appreciate God's majesty through tinted windows in the backseat of the minivan while en route to the next activity. I wanted my children to notice a rainbow in the sky or catch lightning bugs and marvel at their unique design. I wanted them to lie on the driveway at night and stare up at the stars and wonder about the things of God. I wanted them to put down the video game controllers and walk along a creek bed and gather up pretty rocks. Or to take the time to sit on the porch swing on the back deck and listen to the birds chirping while the squirrels chase each other on a labyrinth of oak tree branches. Never before has it been more important to expose our children to God's majesty than it is today when they are tethered to devices filled with man-made distractions that bid for their attention around the clock.

An article in *Ladies Home Journal* entitled "Today's Overscheduled Kids" states that the problem of overcommitment is so serious that "some experts want to see stress-management programs, already offered in some schools, taught from elementary through high school." These same experts emphasize that "the only real solution may be for parents to make major changes in their kids' lifestyles—and their own."[1] Stress-management programs in the schools? Give me a break! Seems to me, it would be a better use of school funds to put the parents in counseling and put an end to this nonsense.

The Authority on Busyness

Jesus is our ultimate example when it comes to ordering our priorities in the midst of busyness. In Mark 1, Jesus lived through a day that makes our busiest days look boring. He started the day by teaching in the synagogue. While he was teaching, a man approached with an unclean spirit (the man was possessed). Jesus cast the spirit out of the man and immediately left the synagogue to head over to the house of Simon and Andrew. (Now, let me pause for a minute and say that most all of us would head to the back bedroom and take to the bed after casting out a demon. A nap would definitely be in order. But a nap was not on Jesus' schedule that day.) When he got to the house, Simon's mother-in-law lay ill with a fever. Jesus healed her and by sundown, "the whole city was gathered together at the door" (Mark 1:33 ESV) wanting in on the deal. Jesus went on to heal many who were sick and cast out demons (Mark 1:21–34). Talk about a long day at the office.

At the very least, you would think he would sleep late the next morning, but he did not. Mark 1:35 tells us, "And rising very early in the morning, while it was still dark, he departed and went out to a desolate place, and there he prayed" (ESV). Jesus knew when it was time to refuel, and he knew what it looked like to truly do so. Have you learned how to identify the time when you need to refuel? Have you designated time to do so? And perhaps even more importantly, have you cultivated the ability to refuel by going to God and not some other empty pursuit? Have you modeled the importance to your family? Jesus knew when it was time to say, "Enough is enough," put the busyness aside, and reconnect with God.

Technology now affords us the ability to be connected around the clock every minute of the day. While this may have some benefits, I'm pretty sure this is not a good thing for our spiritual lives. With all the white noise, we are missing the blessing of silence and solitude. It's in the still, quiet places where God often speaks his truths into our hearts. Jesus sought out a desolate place apart from the crowd, apart from even his friends. If we are to find a desolate place, we must be willing to unplug from our friends and the crowd. Can you imagine Jesus pouring out his heart to God with the buzz of a cell phone going off in his pocket? Or with the chatter from a television in the background? One of the greatest challenges our children will face will be learning to unplug from the white noise and tune in to the things of God. We must lead the way by our example. This problem is too important to ignore.

If you feel the constant barrage of technology is distracting you (or your children) from spending time alone with God, consider implementing some disciplines in your home that encourage designated times to unplug. For example, have a basket in the kitchen where everyone is required to dump their phones during the dinner hour or other designated family times. Encourage your children to start their day with a few minutes of silence and solitude. Many people access their devotionals or Bibles on their phones, so even designated quiet times can be interrupted by "the crowd." If this is a problem for your family, you might consider going back to a hard copy or using another device that won't buzz with calls, texts, or e-mail notifications. Our time spent engaging in technology may not seem like a form of busyness, but when you add up the sum total of unscheduled interruptions that bid for our time each day, it is an activity that must be addressed.

Extracurricular Overload

If we are to tackle the problem of busyness, we must address the world's lie that good mothers expose their children to every activity under the sun. I took a ride on that particular crazy train, and I'm still apologizing to my adult children for not getting off sooner. I understand the pressure you are under. Been there, done that. I've not only heard the justifications; I've said them at the height of my insanity: "How will they know what their gifts are unless I expose them to a variety of activities?" "I want them to grow up to be well-rounded adults." "It's competitive out there, and a padded résumé may set them apart from other college applicants." "I like to keep them busy so they don't have time to get into trouble." Blah, blah, blah.

I remember sitting in a small group when my oldest two kids were three and one and feeling the first wave of pressure to jump on the extracurricular bandwagon. A mother in the group shared how her daughter (age four) was on the waiting list for Suzuki violin lessons and asked if we would add it to the list of prayer requests. She then proceeded to enlighten the rest of the group about the proven benefits of learning to play the violin at an early age. I'm pretty sure it secured early admittance to Harvard and led to the Nobel Peace Prize for inventing a cure for cancer. After she played in Carnegie Hall, of course. In that moment, I recall feeling panicked that my poor children were treading a pathway to average. It was time to step up my game. And with that, the rat race began: T-ball, soccer, piano, guitar, drama camp, gymnastics, dance class, competitive cheerleading, football, basketball, baseball—you name it, and we've probably tried it.

Every year, we packed the calendar with after-school activities sandwiched in between mounds of homework. I learned to write books from my minivan or while sitting in the bleachers on a Little League field waiting for a game to begin. Summers were a tailspin of half-day summer camps, swim lessons, and church activities. We adapted to the pace, and before we knew it, it became a way of life. Busyness was all we knew. Every now and then, I would run across some rebel mother who refused to jump into the fray of breakneck busyness. You know, the mother who—when approached to sign her child up for culinary camp at the community rec center—would confidently reply, "We're going to pass. We're at our limit right now with swim lessons and VBS." Yeah, *that mother*. Aren't you killing two birds with one stone if you can get your kids out of the house AND put them in charge of the family meal after culinary camp? Do they have a laundry camp too? Sign the Courtney kids up!

But, deep down inside, I wanted to be that rebel mother who could say "no" to the buffet of extracurricular activities that all the other mothers were adding onto their already over-crowded plates. I desperately wanted sane. I longed for simple. And I was determined to get it or die trying. Learning to say "no" for myself was only the first step. The next step was to quit the family busyness. It was time to hand in my notice.

Rewriting the Family Busyness Plan

Scripture reminds us, "'Everything is permissible for me'—but not everything is beneficial. 'Everything is permissible for me'—but I will not be mastered by anything" (1 Cor. 6:12 NIV). It's time to come up with a new plan when we reach a point where we are enslaved to busyness. The only way to turn a profit in the family busyness is to make sure you manage the busyness rather than allow the busyness to manage you. At the end of the day, you are in charge of the family calendar and the only one who can make the necessary changes.

If your family is running on fumes and God has gotten nudged out of the center in the process, it's time for a new busyness plan. Sit your family down and be honest with them. Tell them you've come to the realization that the family has gotten off track and is mastered by the calendar rather than by God. There is nothing wrong with admitting your mistakes to your children (within reason, of course). It will serve as a reminder that you're not perfect and give them permission to own their mistakes and failures in the future. If your children are old enough, consider including them in the process of cutting activities from the calendar.

One of the best family decisions we ever made was when we decided to impose a limit of one extracurricular activity per child/per season. Trust me, it was still chaotic at times but nothing like it had been before. My only regret is that we didn't do it sooner. Your kids may balk at first, but I promise you, they will eventually adjust to the saner pace in your home.

What needs to be eliminated from your family calendar to free up space and time to truly cultivate healthy relationships with God? Do your children really need to be in multiple activities or clubs at the same time? Do they need to have an extracurricular activity every single season? If you are living in your car most every day and home has become the place where you crash at night before you wake up and begin the cycle of insanity all over again, it's time for a change. Or maybe it's not extracurricular activities that need to be eliminated from your calendar—maybe you need to delegate more of the duties to your children. Are you overmanaging your children to the point you do most everything for them? Author Robert Heinlein said, "Don't handicap your children by making their lives easy."[2]

Are you the mother who double-checks your child's homework assignments before they turn them in the following day? Do you do your child's laundry? Fold their clothes? Pack their lunch? Iron their shirts? Do you pick up after your child? Make their haircut appointments for them? Oh sure, our kids need help when they are young, but many of us fail to hand over these duties when they are old enough to handle the responsibility. Many of us enjoy loving on our children by doing for them, but do we need to do *everything* for them? In doing so, we rob them of the ability to feel the gratification that comes from a sense of accomplishment.

My husband did an amazing job at giving our children chores at a very young age. My children were doing their own laundry when they were small enough to need a stool in front of the washing machine in order to reach the dial. They took turns doing the dishes, yardwork, trash duty, and other regular duties around the house. And yes, of course they complained and told us we were the meanest parents in the world. Today, as grown adults, they have thanked us for being their *parents* rather than their *personal assistants*.

One area where I had to learn to let go was when it came to image maintenance. It was a full-time job to make sure my children left the house looking neat and kempt with their clothes ironed, hair combed, and teeth brushed. For example, I was in a constant battle with my oldest son over his hair throughout his middle and high school years. He had curly hair, which had to be cut often in order to look tame and manageable. Every four to six weeks, I was on him to call and make an appointment to get his hair cut. You'd think I was asking him to schedule a dentist appointment to have teeth pulled. I nagged. He resisted. I nagged some more.

At some point along the way (unfortunately, it was later than sooner), I realized that I needed to choose my battles and this wasn't one of them. As a result, we have family pictures on display in our home where my son's hair was so bushy, it could justify its own zip code. Now, as a grown young man, my son sees the pictures and asks, "Why didn't you make me get my hair cut?!" Go figure. I'm especially looking forward to the day when he has children old enough to shame him mercilessly about his hair-helmet in the pictures. What a sweet day that will be!

Every family is different, and only you and our husband are qualified to know what needs to be eliminated from the calendar or where you can cut corners to redeem a more simple life. Pray about it and ask God to show you the areas in your day that can be eliminated or adjusted.

Kid-Centric Homes

In his book *Counterfeit Gods*, Tim Keller reminds us of the elders of Israel in Ezekiel 14:3 who "set up their idols in their hearts." Keller notes: "The human heart takes good things like a successful career, love, material possessions, even family, and turns them into ultimate things. Our hearts deify them as the center of our lives, because, we think, they can give us significance and security, safety and fulfillment, if we attain them."[3] Early on in my parenting, I was definitely guilty of "deifying my children as the center of my life." It is painful for me to admit to that, but it's true.

From the outside, it may appear selfless when parents put the children at the center of their lives, but in truth it's selfish. It's really not about the children—it's about the parents. Their hopes. Their dreams. Their expectations. Mom and/or Dad is looking to the children to deliver the satisfaction and fulfillment they long to receive. God has wired our hearts to seek satisfaction and fulfillment, but he never intended our children to meet that need. God alone satisfies and sustains the human heart, and when we look elsewhere to have that need met, fallout will occur.

Unfortunately, kid-centric homes have become the norm in our culture. In kid-centric homes, parents have abdicated the power to the children in an attempt to be labeled their "buddy" or "friend." In kid-centric homes, parents cave in to their children's demands for expensive electronic gadgets and designer clothes because they don't want their children to feel left out or unpopular. In kid-centric homes, parents wait on their children and handle their daily affairs like unpaid personal assistants. In kid-centric homes, parents fight their children's battles and rescue them from the consequences of poor choices. In kid-centric homes, parents defer to the children's preferences, whether it be a summer vacation destination or what's on the menu for dinner. In kid-centric homes, children are allowed to skip church and youth group activities for weekend club team sports. In kid-centric homes, children grow up assuming it's all about them because their parents have made it all about them. How sad when they leave home and discover the rest of the world disagrees and refuses to worship them!

In God-centric homes, time devoted to God is a priority rather than an afterthought. In God-centric homes, the family bows to God rather than a calendar of activities . . . or worse yet, the children. In God-centric homes, the marriage is prioritized over the children, and date nights are not shoved aside for the children's activities. In God-centric homes, children are taught the value or hard work and service to others. In God-centric homes, children are taught that money is a gift from God and to be used according to his will. In God-centric homes children grow up knowing it's all about God because their parents have made it all about God.

Our actions speak volumes about our affections. Do your actions reflect to your children that Jesus is at the center of your worship? Or do your actions reflect that your children are at the center of your worship? Your first step is to resign from the family busyness and refuse to be a slave to the family calendar (or your children!) for another day. The cycle stops with you. It will be impossible to gain control of the family busyness until you put Jesus in his rightful place.

Notes

1. Patrick Kiger, "Today's Overscheduled Kids." More and more kids—from tots to teens—are overworked and overscheduled, and they're cracking under the pressure in ways that you may not recognize, http://www.lhj.com/relationships/family/raising-kids/todays-overscheduled-kids/?page=1.

2. Robert A. Heinlein, BrainyQuote.com, Xplore Inc, 2012; http://www.brainyquote.com/quotes/quotes/r/robertahe106973.html, accessed September 24, 2012.

Chapter 9

Water with Lemon

When I headed out the door for my first year in college, my father handed me a credit card and told me it was for emergencies only. Unfortunately, we had two different ideas of what constituted an "emergency." Like, for example, when you discover that the outfit you planned to wear to the football game that evening is dirty and all the washing machines in the dorm laundry room are taken. That, my friends, is what we refer to as a "fashion emergency" and a justified reason to head to the nearest shopping mall. As a daddy's girl my explanations regarding my emergency purchases were often tolerated and excused with an eye roll and headshake. And then, I got married. Unfortunately, my husband was not nearly as understanding when it came to my spendthrift ways.

I learned this fact a couple of weeks after our first Christmas when I came home with some Christmas decorations that had been discounted in price. I was so excited to show him my bargain purchases and bragged, "All this stuff was 75 percent off! I saved us so much money!" To which he replied, "You could have saved us 100 percent if you had just stayed at home!" And so was the theme through the years. I bought. He barked. I tried not to buy. Eventually I caved. He barked again. Sometimes, I cried. Especially, if it involved a new pair of shoes. At one point, I declared that the word *budget* was a cuss word as far as I was concerned. I believe in having a budget, but hearing the phrase "It's not in the budget" day after day grows old. And it can drive a person to go to desperate lengths—like hiding purchases in the back of the closet until the monthly credit card statement arrives.

You have never met a more frugal man than my husband. Dave Ramsey calls *him* for advice. OK, not really, but he should. Don't believe me? Here are a few of my husband's most memorable moments of frugality:

1. After I accidentally sideswiped the side mirror on his car while backing out of our driveway, he reattached it with duct tape rather than pay the deductible to have it fixed. He continued to drive the car for a couple of years and

parked it in his law firm's parking garage amid a sea of high-dollar luxury cars.

2. One morning, I caught him eating bacon bits (the kind that come in a bag) with his eggs. He explained that they were about to expire and he didn't want to waste them.

3. I recently reorganized our master closet and discovered he owns nine pairs of shoes. NINE. I own over nine pairs of flip-flops alone.

4. When dining out, Keith felt that the price of soft drinks for a family of five was highway robbery, so unless a drink was included in the price of a kid's meal or it was your birthday, you were getting water with lemon. When the kids were toddlers, he taught them how to make lemonade at the table by squeezing in a couple of lemon wedges and mixing in a packet of sweetener.

Honestly, his frugal ways got under my skin in the early years of our marriage. OK, and the mid to latter years too. I would get frustrated when my friends would get new cars, bigger houses, cute stuff for their kids, or, for that matter, a soft drink at a restaurant. I would harass him about his unwillingness to charge more than we could pay off at the end of each month. "But honey, evreeeeeeeeeyone does it!" At the time, I didn't have any proof to back up my statement, but I have since learned it's pretty much true. The average American household owes over $10,000 in credit card debt. An average of $8,000 of that amount makes up revolving debt, which essentially means a whole lot of couples are spending far more than they make.[1]

Even though living beyond our means has become the norm in our society, the piper will have to be paid someday. Or mortgage company. Or electronics store. Or collection agent. The borrower is a slave to the lender (Prov. 22:7).

In my heart, I knew my husband was the wise one by setting aside money for the future (or unplanned emergencies), but at times I felt like everyone was at the popular kids' party and I wasn't allowed to go. He was the wise ant spoken of in Proverbs who stores its provisions in summer and gathers its food at harvest (Prov. 6:6–8). All I could see was how much fun the sluggards were having at the party, not to mention the darling shoes they were wearing. Bitterness took root and the head-butting continued. I know I sound like a spoiled brat, and at times, I was. In truth, if I had been in charge of the finances, we'd be in trouble. Big trouble. I may have complained, but deep down, it brought me security to know my husband was being a good provider and looking ahead to the future.

Fast-forward about twenty years. My husband and I are sitting across a table from our longtime financial advisor, and he is commending us (insert a soft kick under the table from my husband) for our, ahem, diligence in saving. "You are in a good position for the future." Fast-forward five more years. Sitting across the same table, we hear, "I see no reason why you guys can't loosen up and pursue some of the things you've dreamed about, within reason, of course." We walked out of the meeting, and I threw my arms around my husband and thanked him for his diligence. And then I announced, "You are taking me to dinner tonight—at a NICE restaurant—to celebrate this very good news and we are going to talk about our dreams." And we did. For the record, I ordered iced tea with my meal. He ordered water with lemon. Some things never change!

The truth is, debt is stressful. It shouldn't surprise us that it takes a toll on marriage. In fact, 56 percent of all divorces are the result of financial pressure. More than half of divorced couples say that money was the subject of most of their arguments and a key factor in driving them apart.[2] If you want to guard your marriage, guard your finances. And let me add that I know of plenty marriages where the wife is the frugal one and takes charge of the finances. It's great if both parties possess the frugal gene (yes, I'm convinced you're either born with it or not), but all you need is one in each family and the other one lending support.

Being financially responsible is not terribly complicated. As Christians we should, at the very least, abide by the following three basic principles when we get a paycheck:

1. Pay God first (10 percent tithe or more to your local church and additional offerings as God leads).
2. Invest in your future next (a suggested 10 percent or more into savings—establish a three to six month emergency fund first, and then make short-term and long-term investments, including a retirement fund, such as 401k).
3. With what's left, spend wisely as a godly steward and don't spend more than you make.

If you're up for some extra credit, below is a list of money-saving tips my husband (and sometimes, I) practiced that can lead to some extra money in your pocket and accounts over the years:

- **Limit eating out**, which will not only save you money, but will save you calories! If you both work, take lunch to work rather than eating out. Keith has done this almost daily for the last twenty-five years. He calculated that it has saved roughly about $150 a month, or get this, approximately $45,000 over twenty-five years. Doing so has also been a time-saver. It has allowed him time over the lunch hour to work on his lesson for the Sunday morning Bible study class he teaches in our church. He can also focus on other things that otherwise would have prevented him from spending as much time with the kids and me.

- **When you and your family eat out, take advantage of discounts.** Many restaurants have coupons that are available online or in the mail. Others boast "kids eat free" or other discount nights.

- **Buy used cars and pay cash for them.** When we had teenagers driving—and at one point, owned five cars— all of them had been purchased as used cars, and we only had one car payment.

- **Keep driving your cars long after they're paid off.** The most cost-effective car you can drive is the one you own. The net savings from driving our cars approximately twenty-four to thirty-six months after they're paid off (taking into account sometimes higher repair costs associated with used cars): approximately $50,000.

- **Do not take on any debt unless you know you will have the money to pay it off.** For example, do not take on debt if it is based on the assumption that you or your spouse will get a future raise or a bonus.

- **Do not take on any debt except for a house that is within your budget, and possibly one car.**

- **Do not buy a house based on what the lenders say you can afford.** Keith and I made this mistake on the purchase of our first home (at my urging). I was young, naïve, and fell madly in love with the oversized garden tub in the master bath that looked like it was big enough to swim laps in. After our mortgage payment, bills, and tithe to the church, we had little money left over for anything else. And that garden tub grew less and less appealing the longer we lived in the house. Fortunately, we sold the house after one year and chalked it up to a hard lesson learned. After that, we made sure there was plenty of margin to allow us to enjoy life outside the walls of our home.

- **Only use a credit card for purchases if you can—and will—pay off the balance each month.** Occasionally, we take advantage of merchant credit cards (with no annual fee) that offer a discount off an initial purchase, and we then pay it off the first month. Then we discontinue use of the card. The savings from this practice can be huge since most credit cards have very high interest rates—often in the range of 18 percent to 22 percent—that apply to any unpaid credit card balances.

- **Think and pray before you buy items, especially expensive items.** Before buying any item, evaluate whether you really need it—not whether you merely want it—and whether you can truly afford it. When considering whether you can afford it, think about not only the purchase price but also its upkeep and maintenance costs, which for some items can be more difficult to handle than the purchase price. For expensive items, this evaluation should include:

  - **Practice the twenty-four-hour rule.** Make it a practice not to buy big-ticket items until waiting at least twenty-four hours to allow you time to evaluate the decision. This one has been hard for me to learn, but it's amazing how a period of evaluation can change your perspective of how much you really "need" an item you previously thought you couldn't live without.

  - **Comparison shopping.** Check around and make sure you are getting the best price for the item you are purchasing. Fortunately, comparison shopping is easy to do now due to the Internet. A good source to use is Consumer Reports. In addition, Amazon has reviews of the items they sell.

- **Save on home utilities.** For example, keep air-conditioning around 78 degrees in the summer, and use ceiling fans and other fans to keep cool. Keep the heat around 70 degrees in the winter, and wear sweats or other warm clothes to keep warm. Turn lights off when no one is in a room.
- **Save money on gasoline.** Buy cars that get good gas mileage. Plan your errands so you can get the most done in the least number of miles.

There is no way for me to address all of the money-saving and management principles that are at your fingertips. Fortunately, several organizations offer biblically based money management classes at churches, or are available in book or DVD formats. Examples include Dave Ramsey's "Financial Peace University" and "Managing Our Finances God's Way" by Crown Financial Ministries.

Very rarely do you see a marriage in which both the husband and the wife are on the same page when it comes to finances. There is typically a spender and a saver in every marriage. If you are the frugal one in your marriage and it has caused tension at times, consider sitting down with your husband and explaining the method to your madness. If he knows your money-saving motives are rooted in protecting your marriage along with your future nest egg, he is less likely to view you as the bad guy. Marriage is about support and compromise, so it might be necessary to loosen up every so often for the sake of the marriage—like ordering a soft drink with dinner or buying him that fishing pole he's been wanting.

The most important thing is that you approach your finances as a team.

Today, I am extremely grateful for my husband's commitment to guarding our finances and, in turn, guarding our marriage. Because of my husband's firm resolve not to spend more than we make, we can breathe a sigh of relief as we enter our empty-nest years. But the best part of being good stewards with God's money is that there is more to invest in kingdom causes.

Notes

1. Gallup poll: http://www.cnbc.com/id/35837090/QUIZ_Love_And_Debt.

2. Ibid.

Chapter 10

School Daze

I am convinced that teachers are engaged in a secret conspiracy to make all mothers certifiably crazy by summer break. I wouldn't be the least bit surprised if they get a finder's fee from the state mental hospitals as part of their bonus incentive package. Priority for admittance should be given first to homeroom mothers and PTA officers. I realize that some of you may be a bit hesitant to believe my teacher conspiracy theory, which, of course, means that your children are not yet school-aged. The truth is, teachers begin this "survival of the fittest" experiment in the first week of school. What else can explain the three-dozen required forms (per child) that must be filled out by hand and submitted the following morning? And while we're on the subject of forms, is this really the best time for teachers to include a questionnaire to "better get to know your child" and ask for a detailed bio of their strengths and weaknesses? (Here's what I put in the weakness column: "My child is adversely affected when his mother goes whack over all the paperwork she has to fill out the first night of school.") And let's not forget that those required forms come home on the same day as the school supply list. Or make that lists, plural, if your child is older than grammar school and changes classes throughout the day.

If you didn't crack while filling out the mounds of paperwork, you most certainly will begin to fall apart when you attempt to track down the composite notebook with graphing lines. One year, I had to hit three office supply stores in my search for this elusive item, only to discover it was on the endangered species list of office supplies. I was on the verge of taking a stack of graph paper to the local Kinko's and paying $24 to have them bound together when, alas, another mother hit the jackpot and picked up some extra notebooks for me. I think she got them from a guy who operates the school supply black market from his garage on the bad side of town. His primary customer base, you may wonder? Crazed mothers, of course. The business has been so successful, he's about to start a line of franchises across the country.

Just when I thought I could kick up my heels and sink into my favorite easy chair in celebration of surviving Day One of the back-to-school mayhem, in walks my youngest with an announcement that he has a "family shield" project due the next day. AND he gets five extra bonus points if he brings in three extra boxes of tissues with the project. I might have had the tissues on hand, had I not used them up the day before while bawling my eyes out over trying to find graphing paper. Time to put on a pot of coffee and get to work. After, of course, I made a late-night run to the local drugstore to get construction paper and markers, since I wiped out the emergency stockpile at home to fill the school supply lists the day before.

The Hall of Shame

Unfortunately my son forgot to mention the part about the family shields being on display in the hallway outside of his classroom on Back-to-School Night. I learned this detail the hard way when I arrived at my child's classroom and was greeted by a group of parents oohing and ahhing at the long line of children's projects on the wall. If I had known the projects were going to be displayed for every other parent to see, I would have called up our black-market buddy to see if he had a family shield project he could rent me for a few weeks. My husband and I quickly spotted our son's project. It was sandwiched between two family shields that looked like they were on loan from the Metropolitan Museum of Art. One project was a hand-sewn family shield that doubled as a windsock to hang proudly over their front porch as a permanent reminder to the awesomeness of their kid . . . or mother . . . or whoever made the project. Another one was made out of actual scrap metal and mounted on a small piece of plywood. It looked like it weighed over a hundred pounds, and I wondered if they had to reinforce the wall beams in the school hallway before hanging it. Clearly, this child's mother was a welder with access to a front-loader. And then there was Hayden's project—a montage of haphazardly cut pieces of construction paper mounted on a half sheet of poster board. Bless my boy's sweet heart. Oh, the shame! His poor little project looked like something a first grader would turn in. Oh, but wait, he was a first grader!

I had to pull myself together before entering the classroom. I couldn't let on that I was cracking this early in the game. I needed to at least make it until the schoolwide Thanksgiving feast in November. You know, the one where you're required to cook more food than you normally would for your actual family on Thanksgiving Day. Yeah, that one. I survived Back-to-School Night and postponed my breakdown for late November. I didn't want to lodge a complaint about the school projects and risk being labeled a whiner so early in the school year.

The week of the schoolwide Thanksgiving feast arrived, and I announced to my family that they were on their own, barring any emergencies. I further defined "emergencies" as blood and broken bones and made my way to the kitchen to report for duty. In other words, I was off the clock, and they were free to forage through the pantry and live off Fruit Roll-Ups and root beer all week for all I cared. I'm happy to report that I made my assigned two-dozen rolls from scratch and cooked up a batch of the homeroom mother's sweet Aunt Thelma's cornbread dressing as per the enclosed recipe, and I did it with a smile on my face and a song in my heart. There was no time to fall apart. While the dressing was browning and the rolls were rising, I had to whip up a pilgrim costume for Hayden to wear to the feast, review fifty math-drill cards with him before sunrise, and somehow manage to be nice to my husband and two older children in the process. Is it just me, or have you noticed that the teachers who often assign the projects that require sewing are the young ones who have yet to have any children of their own? Their biggest worry at the end of the day is feeding Mr. Jingles, the house cat, and remembering to pick up the dry cleaning by 5:00 p.m. Father, forgive them, they know not what they do.

Death by School Projects

The pace is crazy enough for parents with one child, but for those of us who have two or more kids in school at the same time, may heaven help us. And I do mean that, literally. You will need heaven's help in order to survive. Take my advice: if you're still in the family planning stages, stagger your kids, oh say, ten years apart to make these years a bit more manageable. That way, the oldest child can raise the younger ones if you get in a pinch (I'm just joking, people, joking!).

I recall a particularly low moment when all three of my kids had a required year-end project due on the same day. (You think the back–to-school mayhem is crazy; it's only a dress rehearsal to prepare you for the end-of-the-year hoopla.) Suffice it to say, we got a bit of a late start on the year-end projects. As in, two-weeks-before-it-was-due-kinda-late-start. Desperate mothers do desperate things, and trust me, I fell into the "desperate mother" category. I delegated the older two children's projects to my husband and turned my attention to my youngest child's rock and mineral project—which coincidentally, just so happened to be the same rock and mineral project his older brother had been assigned five years prior. You know, the one I had put in the attic and saved for, oh say, a rainy day.

Now, before you jump to conclusions and think I just dusted off my older son's project, scratched through his name, and scribbled in my youngest son's name, give me a little credit. I gathered up the rocks and scattered them around the front and backyard. I then had Hayden go on a little rock hunt adventure and find them. After that, I had him identify each one by looking them up in his rock and mineral guide and labeling them accordingly, as per the instructions. Judge me if you want, but he still learned something along the way. And he was one step ahead of his siblings for the backyard egg hunt when Easter rolled around, since I tipped him off to my primo hiding spots. Never mind that he still thinks pink quartzite is native to our backyard.

If the rock and mineral project was a low moment in my grammar school mommy years, the mold project certainly helped me reclaim my lost self-esteem and put me back in the running for Mother-of-the-Year. My daughter's science teacher offered extra credit points to anyone who could present him with an example of mold and only gave two days notice. Of course, Paige didn't bring it up until the night before, but hey, no problema! We opened the fridge and jackpot! We found enough mold samples to supply Paige and her three best friends. Take that, June Cleaver. Poor Beav and Wally would have been out of luck on that extra-credit project. Unless, that is, they happened to be friends with my daughter.

As I reflect back on those crazy, chaotic school years, I remember wondering if I was the only one who was struggling to keep up with the pace. I would run into other mothers who seemed so calm, cool, and collected. Were they just better actresses when it came to hiding the nervous tic brought on by the school-daze frenzy? Was there stress in their marriage related to the pace? Were they crumbling behind closed doors in the privacy of their own homes? Of course, in hindsight, I'm sure they thought I was among the calm, cool, and collected as well.

Yet, when I read through the Proverbs 31 passage, I see a similar chaotic pace in play. The virtuous woman was buying vineyards, sewing bed coverings, selling sashes to the merchant ships, and reaching out to the needy. And on top of that, she was doing her husband good and not harm, all the days of her life. All of them? Every single one? We get a glimpse into her attitude in verse 25: "Strength and dignity are her clothing, and she laughs at the time to come" (ESV). Aha, maybe we're onto something here. She accepted the chaos that fell outside of her control with a calm attitude of "It is what it is." The truth is, you can't laugh at the time to come until you first learn to laugh at the day at hand. At the end of the day, we're all just doing the best job we possibly can to survive the whirlwind of school-daze activity. There are some things we can scale back on (ahem, such as recycling rock and mineral projects) in order to lighten the load and make it a more manageable pace. Most importantly, we need to cut ourselves some slack when it comes to the pressure we feel to measure up to an impossible standard to do everything and do it perfectly.

I am reminded of the two sisters Mary and Martha who are spoken of in Luke 11. While Mary sat at the feet of Jesus and listened to his teaching, Martha "was distracted with much serving" (Luke 10:40 ESV). At one point, she appealed to Jesus to tell her sister to come and help her. She basically tattled on her sister. Jesus didn't exactly give her the answer she was hoping for and instead told her: "Martha, Martha, you are anxious and troubled about many things, but one thing is necessary. Mary has chosen the good portion, which will not be taken away from her" (Luke 41–42 ESV). We've all had our

Martha moments. Distracted, worn out, tired, weary, always doing, doing, doing. But are we doing *too much*? If we are missing out on the one thing needed, we most certainly are. One Bible commentary notes that "whereas Martha was in care to provide many dishes of meat, there was occasion but for one, one would be enough."[1] Jesus was addressing the problem of overkill. Too often, we bring more to the table than is necessary when it comes to helping our children prosper. Maybe we should aim for *enough* rather than *too much*.

A Healthy Perspective

I am grateful for the Scripture's instructions about raising children that can give us perspective during the more chaotic moments that arise in the parenting journey. Deuteronomy 6 talks about teaching our kids to love God and love others. The book of Proverbs is full of admonition to discipline. Ephesians reminds fathers not to provoke their children to anger. I am also grateful for what Scripture does NOT say about being a parent. There is nothing in Scripture about being a perfect parent. There is no Thirteenth Commandment about making sure your children's school projects look professionally tailored. There is no lower level of heaven reserved for parents whose children only make Cs. And praise God, he didn't base our salvation on whether or not our children win a ribbon at the science fair.

A Scripture that is surprisingly helpful for parents in the trenches of school daze comes from the Psalms: "Our lives last seventy years or, if we are strong, eighty years. Even the best of them are struggle and sorrow; indeed, they pass quickly and we fly away" (90:10 HCSB). Translation: Time flies. Our lives are short. The things that matter so much to us in this moment, like the best pilgrim costume ever seen on any child in the state of Texas, won't really matter twenty years from now. That project you're flipping out over? It'll be in the trash can by the end of the year. (Unless you decide to sell it on the black market!) This Scripture is a reminder of perspective—get some and keep it.

If you're currently in the midst of the school daze, I want you to take a breath. And now, try to crack a smile. Even if it's forced. Breathe. Smile. Repeat. After a while, it will come more naturally. You're doing a great job. No one has it all down. We're all just taking it one day at a time, one pilgrim costume at a time, one late-night-trip-to-the-craft-store at a time. Even those of us writing the parenting books. Take a pat on the back from this empty nester who today is laughing her head off at the memory of it all. And wishes she had started laughing sooner in the game. This, too, shall pass. And in the meantime, give me a buzz if you need a rock and mineral project, family shield, or pilgrim costume. I might be able to set you up. ∼☺

Notes

1. Matthew Henry, *Commentary on the Whole Bible—New Testament* (Nashville: Thomas Nelson, 2003).

Chapter 11

Circle the Bandwagons

Ask the average mother what her deepest desire is for her children, and you will likely hear an answer that contains the words *happy* and *healthy*. Ask a Christian mother and she will likely add a tagline about "loving Jesus." Mothers feel a deep sense of responsibility when it comes to the future happiness, success, health, and spiritual well-being of their children. Because of our deep desire to see our children prosper, we are easy prey to parenting trends, books, and products that promise to give our children a guaranteed edge in the game of life. While you're at it, let's go ahead and add grandmothers to that list as well. While on a recent trip to Costco, I caved in and bought my grandson a value pack of Baby Einstein toys, and as you might have guessed, he ended up preferring the boxes the toys came in over the toys themselves.

When it comes to bandwagons, Baby Einstein has seen its share of glory days. The creators of the Baby Einstein line of toys began with a series of educational videos in 1997. They could never have predicted at the time that their little foray would morph into The Baby Einstein Company, a multimillion-dollar enterprise. In 2001 they sold the company to Disney. But here's where it gets interesting. Eight years later, in 2009, Disney offered a refund of up to $15.99 per household to families who purchased the Baby Einstein videos because the videos weren't actually making children any smarter![1] Disney was likely responding to threats of a class-action suit for unfair and deceptive marketing practices. The marketing strategy for the Baby Einstein videos was based on implied claims that the videos are "educational and beneficial for early childhood development."

Parents bought into the marketing bait hook, line, and sinker. A 2003 study revealed that a third of all American babies from six months to two years of age have at least one Baby Einstein video, which means that a whole lot of parents hopped on the Baby Einstein bandwagon. Until, that is, another study revealed that children who are exposed to television between the ages of one and three develop attention problems by the age seven. Not only are the videos without any benefits for our little munchkins, they may actually put them at a disadvantage. At the end of the day, plopping your baby in front of Baby Einstein videos is no more effective when it comes to influencing future intelligence than exposing them to the evening news.

Guilt Tactics

The Baby Einstein phenomenon is a great example of the "bandwagon effect." Wikipedia defines the "bandwagon effect" as a "form of groupthink." As the fad or trend begins to catch on and spread, more and more people "hop on the bandwagon" regardless of the underlying evidence.[2] And there is no shortage of bandwagons to jump on when it comes to parenting trends. A mother is particularly susceptible to bandwagons that tap into her deepest fears, especially fears related to her children.

While recently cleaning out my office bookshelves, I stumbled upon a nutrition book related to sugar intake. I'd picked it up back in the late '90s. I brushed off the dust from the book while taking a swig of my sugary soda and tossed the book into the garage-sale box. In my defense, I was successful in eliminating sugar from my family's diet for a full two weeks until my husband and children staged a full-blown mutiny and called a halt to the sugar-free insanity. One of the kids had an upcoming birthday party and vetoed my proposed menu of carrot sticks and tofu cake. I had no choice but to put the book on a shelf and hand over their Toaster Strudels. At the end of the day, my family loves sugar too much to trade it in for a gain of ten years added to their average lifespans. Like my father-in-law says, "Those last few years ain't so swift anyway."

I can't recall what exactly prompted my sugar-free bandwagon, but I remember seeing the author on an afternoon talk show and falling prey to the sales pitch. Who wouldn't crater after forty-five minutes of doom and gloom statistics, complete with a tabletop sampling of crystallized organs belonging to sugar-crazed cadavers? You'd think I would have learned my lesson after the last nutrition bandwagon when I swore off store-bought strained baby food, opting instead to make it myself (firstborn child, of course). I decided to ditch the store-bought stuff after hearing a presentation by a nutritionist that had been invited to speak at a Mothers of Preschoolers small group. In summary, store-bought baby food = BAD. As in, sign your baby up for community college because their poor little brains are atrophying by the minute with every little bite of Gerber goodness you spoon into their eager mouths. And you, dear mother, will be to blame.

The nutritionist also taught us how to read the labels on canned foods while grocery shopping because, Lord knows, every mother has time for that when your three kids are tossing Double-Stuffed Oreos and Froot Loops into the basket at warp speed. I think her point amounted to, "Don't bother grocery shopping because everything in the supermarket is of the devil. Plant a garden and eat what you grow, young, naïve hippie mothers." By the end of the presentation, I practically knocked the other mothers to the ground as I raced out the door and headed to the store to purchase a mini food processor and fresh fruits and veggies. At this point, my poor kids had consumed enough processed and packaged foods to put their future SAT scores into the negative digits. Instantly, I got a mental image of my three children lying on a black sofa in a counselor's office as they shared the domino effect of being raised on store-bought baby food. After, of course, they processed the emotional devastation of having a mother who didn't scrapbook.

As you may have guessed, the make-your-baby-food-from-scratch phase lasted just long enough for me to figure out that (1) my youngest would be eating finger foods by the time I finished making the first batch; and (2) the end result would taste so bland, he would tongue-thrust every precious bite out of his mouth. When this happened, I wanted to scoop up every discarded bite and refreeze them until I could incorporate them into a Thanksgiving dinner casserole. I had spent more time making this batch of baby food than any other dish I had ever prepared in my life. Someone was going to enjoy this baby food if I had to eat it myself for breakfast, lunch, and dinner. In the end, I mixed it into my dog's canned food and she even snubbed it. Ultimately, I determined that my mental health was of far greater importance than such nuanced aspects of my children's physical health. I ask you, what good are the long-term benefits of homemade baby food if Mama goes cray-cray in the process of making it from scratch? Bandwagon officially over. Until, of course, Y2K came along and my stockpiling-for-Armageddon frenzy resulted in a three-year supply of bottled water and beef jerky. Fortunately, my boys are huge fans of beef jerky, so all was not lost.

My kids are adults now, and I'm happy to say they are healthy, happy, and had no problems getting into college, in spite of their sugary, processed diets. In fact, my youngest child (who by default of being the youngest and raised on whatever junk food he could find in the pantry) somehow managed to score a perfect eight hundred on the math portion of the SAT on his first try. I was seriously tempted to track down the mailing address of the nutritionist who had guilted me about store-bought baby food and send her a copy of his scores with a Post-it Note saying something like "Child raised on store-bought baby food. P.S. I loaded him up on chocolate milk and frozen Eggo waffles on the morning of the SAT exam rather than the recommended nutritious breakfast." I think we're onto something here, people.

I'm certainly not knocking a mother's commitment to feeding her children nutritious foods, especially in a culture where so many kids are overweight. I'm warning against an over-the-top, extreme devotion to parenting bandwagons that send a conflicting message to our children that our devotion to the cause is more important than our devotion to Christ and eternal matters. Colossians 3:2 reminds us, "Set your minds on things that are above, not on things that are on earth" (ESV). Whether the end goal is nutrition, academics, athletic pursuits, or any other noble goal we may have in mind, our ultimate priority is to point our children to a loving God and to seek him above all else.

Spiritual Bandwagons

When I found out I was expecting my first child, I could hardly wait to be a mother. I read books, set up a nursery, and prepared as best I could for the transition into parenthood. But nothing could prepare me for the bully moms I would encounter in the months that followed my son's birth. Oh, you've met Bully Mom. This is the mother who takes a controversial issue and makes it her personal mission to "preach" her personal opinion as the gospel truth, derailing all others who dare to oppose. I recall sitting around a table in a small group for Mothers of Preschoolers as a naïve, new mother when I had my first encounter with a bully mom. You name a topic, and this mom had an opinion on it. And trust me, you would hear that opinion whether you wanted to or not.

Her arsenal of hot-button topics included breast-feeding versus bottle-feeding; spanking or not spanking; stay-at-home moms versus working moms, and, of course, the evils of daycare. This woman was relentless. I was a young, impressionable mother who was already struggling with insecurities, so her rants often sent me into a tailspin of self-doubt. To complicate matters even further, I was a fairly new believer, and her rants were at times seasoned with vague Scriptures and references to a popular Christian movement that was sweeping through many churches in the '80s. The specific movement isn't the point because it seems each generation finds a different way to manifest these tendencies. She would attribute all of the "should dos" and "oh gracious, never dos" to the leader of the movement whom she cited with an air of authority. And trust me, the leader of that particular group had a lot of opinions on everything from marriage to parenting to living the Christian life in general. He even threw in some bonus opinions related to Christian rock music (bad) and Cabbage Patch dolls (don't ask).

A few of my friends jumped on that particular bandwagon and embraced much of this man's teaching related to marriage and family. Some got bossy about their beliefs, while others were more respectful. Many of the most outrageous, fringe teachings were not adopted by his mainstream following, and I imagine that was a contributing factor to the movement (bandwagon) eventually losing steam.

I'm certainly not saying that there wasn't merit to some of the things taught in that movement. In fact, I have friends who still speak very highly of his teachings related to certain practices. They were able to apply more of a cafeteria-style approach to the teachings, embracing some principles but disregarding others. My concern is for those who don't have the same ability to discern the good from the bad. I've often seen that women are particularly susceptible to strong opinions, especially when it plays into natural fears we have about the well-being (physical, emotional, and spiritual) of our children. Scripture warns of this tendency in 2 Timothy 3:6–7 when it advises Christians to be on the lookout for those "who creep into households and capture weak women, burdened with sins and led astray by various passions, always learning and never able to arrive at a knowledge of the truth" (ESV). The context of this passage is speaking about the last days, which none of us can truly know is now or not, but ultimately the principle to be on guard against such things is one that is always applicable!

There will always be those in the faith who would rather subscribe to someone else's teaching than go directly to God's Word for the answers. For this reason, we need to learn to be critical thinkers and, more importantly, avid students of God's Word. Many spiritual bandwagons begin as sincere, God-centered movements led by sincere, God-fearing individuals. However, it's easy to take a turn off the main road and begin to look to a leader for answers rather than running straight to the Source for questions. As followers of Jesus, we always need to ask, "What does God's Word really say about this?"

It's hard enough to be a mother as it is, so let's agree to offer grace to other mothers who don't embrace our same beliefs when it comes to the gray areas of parenting. I'm stepping on my own toes, here. I've had my moments in which I've been the bully mom and have taken a legalistic high road on certain topics I'm passionate about. Over the years, God has convicted my heart that my presentation has at times lacked compassion and grace. I have since come to the conclusion that God is fully capable of convicting a fellow believer's heart without me butting in and trying to do his job for him.

I've also learned that what's right for me and my family is not always God's will for someone else's family. I've also had moments where God has clearly shown me that a particular issue is not as black-and-white as I had imagined it to be. It's a lot easier to label something as good or bad. It is much harder to accept and live with the ambiguity of issues that aren't clearly defined by Scripture. Living without answers requires that we leave the answers up to God, something with which we all struggle. We want to define, control, and dictate our world.

The truth is, there will always be another bandwagon waiting around the corner. Some may be worth our time, while others will do nothing more than distract us from more important matters—eternal matters. Ecclesiastes 1:9 reminds us of the futility of parenting bandwagons, "History merely repeats itself. It has all been done before. Nothing under the sun is truly new" (NLT). When we hop on a bandwagon, we need to remember that it's not a solo experience. We sign our entire family up for the ride. For this reason, we need to be careful about what we pour our time and passion into and be leery of extremes. You've heard the saying, "All things in moderation," and the same is true for many of the parenting bandwagons we are quick to hop on. Moderation is the key. And making sure you know when it's time to hop off the bandwagon. ～⌖

Notes

    1. See http://www.parentdish.com/2009/10/26/disney-offers-refunds-for-baby-einstein-videos.

    2. See http://en.wikipedia.org/wiki/Bandwagon_effect.

Chapter 12

Merry Christmas from the Stepford Family

I love Christmas. When it comes to family togetherness and making memories, there is no better time of year. I'm one of those Christmas freaks who puts up the decorations the day after Thanksgiving and not a day later. I love Christmas shopping and hearing the Christmas songs on the radio and in the stores. And I especially enjoy receiving Christmas cards. Barring one card, that is. You probably get the same card. I'm talking about the one with the fleur-de-lis hand-stamped monogram return address from none other than . . . the Stepford family. Oh, that's not their real name, but you know who I'm talking about. No one can escape the Stepfords' annual Christmas letter—or, as I like to call it, the "my-kids-are-better-than-your-kids letter." Yes, that family. Perfect. Polished. Prim. Proper. Chances are, you get a handful of these letters each year, and at least one in the bunch makes you grumble under your breath before you ever reach the second paragraph.

Reading the Stepfords' annual Christmas letter produces instant guilt. You are going to hear all about their precious little Johnny, who's only five years old and can speak Spanish fluently (thanks to the full-time housekeeper, Consuela). But that's not all. He also knows his multiplication tables, and is already receiving college recruitment letters from Harvard and Yale. And if the letter alone is not enough to put you in guilt-overload, the enclosed picture of Mom, Dad, and their perfectly groomed little Lord Fauntleroy will most likely do the trick. Never mind that you finish reading the letter just in time to see your own five-year-old little cherub wiping a booger on your crisp, white linen tablecloth (the one that was ironed by you and not a full-time housekeeper named Consuela) as he rushes through the kitchen with his shoes on the wrong feet. Community college, here we come.

Actually, I don't have much room to talk or point fingers. I have written an annual Christmas letter (with picture included) every year, beginning when my oldest child was only six months old. Guilty as charged. To date, we have an album of over two decades worth of annual Christmas letters documenting the yearly Courtney family highlights in review. While recently flipping through the album to read some of the earlier letters, I cringed at things I had written in the earlier editions. The letters weren't quite as obnoxious as the example I mocked above, but they definitely bordered on braggadocious and left me wanting to crawl into a hole. Did no one in my family love me enough to stage an intervention and seize my embellished holly-berry stationery?

Did I really tell my readers in 1988 that my six-month-old son, Ryan, was chosen to play the part of baby Jesus in the church Christmas musical because he had the most Christlike temperament in the church nursery? I said it tongue in cheek, but deep down inside, I'm pretty sure I thought it was true. Or how about the year I disclosed (bragged?) that my daughter, Paige, was the youngest member of the Tiny Tots gymnastics class to be bumped up to the next level after having mastered a series of dive rolls down the mat? Ugh. And then there was the year Hayden was born, and I somehow felt a need to share (boast?) how many jars of baby food he could consume in the course of a day. Because mercy, everyone knows it will enrich the lives of my friends to know that interesting bit of trivia. Or consider this one (possibly one of my top ten worst): "Ryan (age six) was recently promoted up to three digit carries in addition and has memorized Psalm 139, Psalm 100, and 1 Corinthians 13." Good Lord, reading that sentence makes me want to go back in time and slap myself silly. I'm surprised I didn't get any removal requests from friends after that edition went out. Or at the very least, a few requests for Ryan to fill in as a guest preacher when the pastor is on vacation.

Truth or Dare

Fortunately, as the kids got older and the insanity level in our house increased, the boasting in the letters, by default, began to decrease. Having three kids in a span of five short years forces you to see life through a more realistic lens—you know, the one smeared with toddler fingerprints and grape jelly. It was the cold slap in the face I needed to come off my gloating high horse. I could either pretend my kids were perfect, or I could be honest and write about such things as Hayden's uncanny ability to belch to the tune of "Happy Birthday," a talent he insisted on displaying at every birthday party he attended. Or how about Ryan conning his younger siblings into spending their hard-earned birthday money to buy rocks he gathered from the front yard for a mere $6 each? (Think grammar school ponzi scheme here.) Or then there was the school function our family attended where classical music was playing in the background, and my daughter, Paige, announced to the headmaster, "This place could use a little rock 'n roll. I'm tired of this stuff." Sigh. I eventually chose to be real rather than put on a plastic smile—and that definitely had an impact on the Christmas letters I wrote. I decided that being honest and vulnerable takes a lot less energy than keeping every hair in place and every child in line.

And a funny thing happened. The more honest I became, the more feedback I got from my readers that they enjoyed and looked forward to reading my annual Christmas letter each year because it promised to be real and honest. Hearing that my children fight nonstop and that the three-year-old somehow picked up the phrase, "toopid, tinky, bu'head" somehow gave hope to my friends. Nevermind that he chose to unleash it at the top of his lungs one day when the windows were open and the neighbors were barbecuing outside. Being honest and real fostered a universal comradery—that we're all in this together, and if we don't find a way to laugh about it, we'll end up crying though the next dozen or so years. My newfound transparency was clearly evident by 1995 (the kids were seven, five, and two years) when I opened my annual letter with a behind-the-scenes look at the events that had transpired in our attempt to get a decent family picture to go along with the letter. Here is what I said:

> Merry Christmas from the Courtney family! I'm not sure many of you realize what a challenge it is to provide you with a photo of my seemingly cherubic and obedient children, but we just may spend 1996 in family counseling to recover from this event alone. First, the children had to be bribed with much candy (yes, we're those kind of parents) before they would agree to put on their fancy duds on a nonchurch day.

Next, Ryan informed me that his shirt was "dorky," which launched me into the "we shouldn't care about what others think" lecture. He responded by rolling his eyes and quickly putting his shirt on in order to bring this familiar lecture to an end. Paige followed by insisting she wear her hair in a "Pocahontas braid" (or to be a bit more politically correct: "Native American braid"). I prevailed by calmly assuring her if she wore her hair down for the picture, she could shave her head when we were finished and go live with Pocahontas, for all I cared.

Once I started writing with a bit more transparency and honesty, I began to hear encouragement from friends, "Have you ever thought about writing before?" I have no doubt that God used the annual Christmas letters to teach me a few lessons about humility, but God also used those letters to serve as a springboard to bigger writing projects that followed. To this day, I continue to hold to the original lesson he taught me in writing those Christmas letters whether I'm working on a book or preparing a speaking message: Keep it real. Resist the urge to play the Stepford family pretender game. At the end of the day, we're all struggling sinners, even if we present ourselves and/or our families in a way that suggests we have it all together.

One of my favorite life verses is Philippians 1:6 which says, "And I am certain that God, who began the good work within you, will continue his work until it is finally finished on the day when Christ Jesus returns" (NLT). He's not finished with us yet. We are all a work in progress. Why are we so afraid to admit to that truth? One Bible commentary notes, "Out of Christ, the best saints are sinners, and unable to stand before God. There is no peace without grace. Inward peace springs from a sense of Divine favour. And there is no grace and peace but from God our Father, the fountain and origin of all blessings."[1] Transparency and humility are not problems when we acknowledge that any good in us is the result of God's grace and mercy.

Paul offers a timely reminder about honesty in Romans 12:3 (NLT): "Because of the privilege and authority God has given me, I give each of you this warning: Don't think you are better than you really are. Be honest in your evaluation of yourselves, measuring yourselves by the faith God has given us." When we succumb to playing the pretender game and only allow others to see the cherry-picked Stepford moments (some even staged), we miss the opportunity to share life with others on a deeper, more meaningful level. Similar to when we are asked casually by a friend, "Hey, how have you been?" and we volley back a default "Great!" Yet in truth everything is falling apart behind the scenes. Maybe God positioned that friend to be a source of encouragement and comfort to us in our time of need. We miss opportunities to be encouraged in times of difficulty when we pretend everything is just fine.

I'm certainly not suggesting that we forego the polished family Christmas photos, opting instead for a more realistic snapshot of our lives. I do, however, regret that I did not send out this particular shot of my children to accompany our annual Christmas letter in 1995:

Talk about a Christmas pic photo shoot gone bad. If this picture doesn't scream "reality" or "work in progress," I'm not sure what does. At the very least it would have made most everyone receiving it breath a huge sigh of relief that they are not alone. When we are able to offer a more "honest evaluation" of ourselves and our families, we free others up to do the

December 1995

same. Life is hard. Parenting is a challenge. Faith is messy. Let's stop pretending it's not. I'm not suggesting we broadcast the unattractive details of our lives, but rather, we resist the temptation to polish everything up and pretend everything is OK. That charade is hard enough to pull off when your children are young, but it's nearly impossible when your children hit the teen years. Parents who insist on playing the pretender game will run themselves ragged trying to do damage control when their children mess up. And trust me, they will.

I recall a phone call I received a few years back from a mother of a girl who attended the same private school as my youngest son. She shared that her daughter (a darling Christian girl) had a little bit of a crush on my son. The mother went on to say she couldn't be more "thrilled" because she had read my books and knew my son must be a fine, Christian young man. Oh boy. The problem was sometimes my son was a fine, Christian young man, and other times, he wasn't. And this just happened to be one of those times when he was chasing after many of the world's pleasures. Rather than play along and "pretend" my son was a good candidate for her daughter, I leveled with her and told her it would be in the best interest of her daughter to steer clear of my son! I could tell she was a bit shocked initially, but I felt such relief in being able to be honest about the situation. Just because I've written a few parenting books, didn't mean my children were exempt when it came to the standard temptations. My three children are as flawed as the parents who raised them.

A Lesson from Bubba

As I flipped through my album of Christmas letters and pictures on a recent afternoon, I could see the time line from "pretender" to "realist" with the passing of each year and each Christmas letter. When I got to the 2004 Christmas letter and picture, I had to laugh out loud. If I had to choose a picture in the album that marked a clear turning point, this would be the one. I had always admired the family beach photos some families would send out from their summer beach vacations. You know, the one where the sun-kissed family is typically standing on a white sand beach, barefoot, of course with the jewel-toned ocean waves in the background. The men and boys are dressed in crisp white shirts while the women and girls wear white linen dresses. If they are from the South, the little girls wear matching white hair bows that are three times the size of their little heads. When I would see a picture like this, I half expected to see Jesus breaking through the clouds in the background and smiling with favor upon the angelic family.

But now, it was my turn. We had planned a summer trip in 2004 to a beautiful white sand beach in Florida, and I was determined to get my first-ever family beach picture. Of course, the goal was to send it out with my end-of-the-year annual Christmas letter. I announced to the family on our last day at the beach that we were going to get a family picture that evening before dinner ~~if they hoped to see the next light of day~~. The announcement was met with a chorus of enthusiastic smiles, high fives, and head nods. Nope. That didn't really happen. As you will see in the picture, my family refused to cooperate with the all-white wardrobe stipulation, opting instead for more of a light Goth-look. I was desperate to get my beach picture, so I bit my lip, and we headed down to the beach. I knew I had about ninety seconds to pull this off before the natives (a.k.a. my sons) got restless and began to suffer withdrawals from the air-conditioned condo and their handheld Game Boy devices. I quickly approached a stranger

on the beach and asked him to snap a few pictures. Mission accomplished, and we were all still speaking to each other when it was over.

It wasn't until I got home from the trip that I noticed the sunburnt Bubba in the background holding a beer koozie and doing a howdy-doody wave. As luck would have it, this particular shot was the only picture where every member of our family had their eyes open and wore expressions that looked vaguely like we liked each other. I had no choice—Bubba had to stay. Look, if anyone was going to look a bit crazed and off in the picture, I'd rather it be Bubba than one of the Courtneys. Of course, this was before digital editing, so I didn't have the option of airbrushing Bubba out.

If a picture's worth a thousand words, this one speaks volumes about the futility of aiming for Stepford-family perfection. It serves as a reminder that there's no such thing as perfect families with perfect smiles who live perfect lives. There's always a Bubba lurking somewhere behind the scenes just waiting to pull back the curtain and expose us for we really are—flawed human beings in need of much grace. Bubba taught us the benefits of learning to laugh at ourselves and how to lighten up a bit when things don't measure up to our high expectations.

So, the next time you receive a too-good-to-be-true Christmas letter from the Stepford family along with a family picture that looks like a photo shoot for a Ralph Lauren catalog, remember that it is only one of many snapshots in the family's life. You are seeing a handpicked, best-of moment. And while you're at it, remember to embrace the Bubbas (well, not literally) when they interrupt your polished plans. You might also want to remember that wearing SPF 50 or above is of critical importance when you go to the beach, or you may end up looking like our friend, Bubba.

Chapter 13

Hold on Loosely

The '80s classic rock song "Hold on Loosely" by 38 Special may have been an ode to a failed relationship, but it offers a snippet of wisdom to parents as well. When a nurse placed my oldest son in my arms for the first time at the hospital, a thousand hopes and fears flooded my mind in that single moment. This tiny little creature was desperately dependent on me. I clutched him tighter at the mere thought. My previous concerns just prior to his birth evaporated in the wake of a new slate of concerns.

Who was that person who just a week ago was worried about finding a coordinating fabric for a window valance that would blend with the nursery palette of colors? For heaven's sake, I had other worries now! There was that scary soft spot to think about. And low-grade fevers that could indicate a serious infection. There was a long lecture from the nurse on how to position him while he slept. (For the record, it was side or stomach but NOT on his back!) I left the hospital with a mountain of paperwork about vaccines, breast-feeding, umbilical cord care, circumcision care, and a safety diagram documenting the correct placement of a car seat, which required a Master's in Engineering to decipher.

My head was spinning with all the details, and for a split second I wondered if it was too late to put him back in the womb. In the weeks that followed, I must have taken the poor kid's temperature a half dozen times per day. I awakened all through the night to double-check, wait, make that triple-check his sleeping position. Fortunately, I didn't have far to go. The bassinet was literally inches from my bed. I eventually began to relax, but a mother's worries never disappear. Little did I know at the time how much easier it was to have my kids right next to me in their bassinets than watch them walk out the front door at the age of sixteen with car keys in hand.

As I looked through the mounds of paperwork and instructions in the days that followed the birth of my first child, I was struck by the fact that there was no instruction manual detailing the general care of my child. It became clear that I was on my own when it came to figuring out how this little creature operates after his umbilical cord falls off. Of course, we know the Bible is our ultimate instruction manual, but where is the passage that gives you step-by-step instructions on what to do when your child runs a fever? Or cries for no reason? Or won't sleep through the night? Oh sure, mothers today have the Internet to help guide them, but I for one, am thankful it wasn't around when my kids were little. I can't tell you how many times I've Googled a symptom and after a brief three minutes of perusing the links been thoroughly convinced I have a brain tumor or cancer. I would have been the mom buzzing the after-hours emergency number at the pediatrician's office on a daily basis after Googling "teething swollen gums" and "splinter in finger" and landing mentally on a worst-possible-scenario link.

For twenty-three years, my days were spent holding onto, hovering over, and eventually, letting go of three precious children entrusted to my care. When you're in the thick of it, it's hard to remember that it's only for a season. At some point, we have to loosen our grip and give them up. They are not ours to keep. That truth became a fresh reality when my husband and I moved our youngest child into his college dorm. We had been on call for twenty-three years, and suddenly the day arrived when it was time to clock out. Oh, he would still come home for the summer breaks and an occasional home-cooked meal (or in my case, Costco meatloaf), but the bulk of our work was done. When we arrived home after the drop-off, it was bittersweet to pull into our empty driveway that just a few years ago looked like a used-car lot. When we walked through the front door, the house was eerily quiet. And just like that, the empty-nest years began.

I'm not going to sugarcoat it. The weeks following college drop-off were hard. I would sometimes forget that he was gone and half expect to see him come down the stairs in the morning, grab his backpack, and head out the door with a quick "love you, Mom." Some evenings, I found myself wondering what was keeping him so long after football practice. And then I would remember: He doesn't live here anymore. When they live under your roof for so many years, it takes time to wrap your mind around the truth that they are gone.

Mourning the Last-Evers

With the onset of the empty-nest years, the weirdest things would catch me off guard and trigger the tears. Walking past my children's bedrooms and seeing the made-up beds . . . that continued to stay made up. Depositing a soda can into the recycle bin in the garage and noticing the wire basket next to it filled with basketballs, footballs, baseball gloves, and other outdoor gear that had provided my children with years of entertainment. Or perhaps, the worst one of all was heading out to dinner with my husband on a Friday night and driving past a high school football stadium where two teams were squaring off for a win. It about sent us over the edge to hear the band playing in the background interrupted by an occasional outburst of cheers from the bleachers. We were no longer a part of that crowd. On graduation day we, too, had graduated along with our children. They got a cap and gown and a new future. We got a quiet house on Friday night.

My husband and I had logged countless hours in the bleachers watching our daughter cheer and our sons play football. If you're from the South, you know that "Friday Night Lights" is not just a season of year but a culture and a way of life. If your child is on the football team, drill team, cheerleading squad, or band, you know the weekend drill. You pack up your stadium chair every Friday night, pin your player pin (a button with your child's picture) on your shirt (with matching team colors), grab your camera, and head to the game. I can still remember my sons' last-ever football game his senior year and the drive home after the game. Out of habit, I unpinned my player pin and put it in its familiar spot in my camera bag. It was then that I remembered the Friday-night-lights chapter was officially over, and the tears began to flow. Again.

Actually, I'm pretty good at mourning the last-ever moments, whether it's a last-ever football game or a last-ever night spent in the baby crib before transitioning to a "big kid bed," or a last-ever day of preschool before gearing up for kindergarten. My husband has often joked that I've been mourning the last-evers since the day our last child was born. Unlike some, I knew my third child would be my last, so I tried to savor the last-evers as they occurred. And by savor, I mean bawl my eyes out.

Most of the last-evers happen without advance warning, and it's not until later that we come to realize one chapter officially ended and another one began. Like when you change your last-ever diaper. Or rock your baby to sleep for the last-ever time. Or make your last-ever bottle or buy your last-ever jar of baby food. . . . You don't know the last-ever time your son will sit in your lap and play with your hair, or the last-ever time your child will take an afternoon nap, or the last-ever time your child will hand you a picture they colored just for you. You don't always know the last-ever Christmas your child will believe in Santa, or the last-ever time your child will crawl into your bed when there's a thunderstorm. . . . Or the last-ever time your daughter will play with her dolls . . . or your son will play with his Hot Wheels. You can't always pinpoint the last-ever time your teenager will ride in your backseat with her posse of friends or the last-ever time she won't mind walking with you in public instead of ten paces in front of you. There's no warning about the last time your daughter will ask you to take her shopping before you are replaced by her best friend who can drive. Mourn these things anyway . . . after the fact, as they come to mind. And celebrate the new chapter that follows.

Some last-evers on the calendar require a stock pile of tissue. Like when I dropped my youngest child off for the first day of kindergarten. After depositing him in his new class, I returned to my car and sobbed buckets of tears as I mourned the last-ever time I would have a child at home with me during the day. Ten minutes and a good cry later, I was better able to celebrate his first-ever day of elementary school. And that was only the beginning of many, many last-evers that required extra tissue—each of my children's homecoming games, senior proms, and high school graduation ceremonies. Here's a hint: a few tears shed in advance did wonders at preventing a full-strength meltdown on the day of. Mourning the last-evers in advance was especially helpful when my oldest son and my daughter each got married within months of each other and spent their last night in their childhood bedrooms on the eve before their weddings. I may have cried for longer than ten minutes for those events.

A Time for Everything

Ecclesiastes 3 reminds us that "for everything there is a season," which includes "a time to weep and a time to laugh, a time to mourn and a time to dance" (Eccl. 3:1, 4 NIV). There is absolutely nothing wrong with mourning the last-evers, assuming of course, the mourning is balanced with a celebration of the first-evers that will follow. In fact, I would argue that shedding a few tears is a healthy way to express the closure of a meaningful and important chapter of your life. While my husband and I experienced moments of sadness when we dropped our last child off to college, we have also been faithful in celebrating the joys (can you say FREEDOM?!) we are experiencing now in the empty-nest chapter of our lives and our son's transition into the adult years.

Celebrate the first-evers, but also give yourself permission to mourn the last-evers. In doing so, you acknowledge the reality that your children will only be in your care for a season. I worry far more about the mothers who ignore this reality, opting instead for ignorance or denial. They will likely find themselves in a world of hurt when the day arrives to say good-bye on the steps of their child's dorm. Trust me, it won't be pretty. I know it's uncomfortable and even sad for many of you to think about that moment when you'll have to say good-bye to your child, but it helps keep our ultimate purpose as mothers in the proper perspective. Our calling from God is a short-term assignment. We are stewards of the moments we have been given to parent them, and that role changes dramatically over the years.

If I had a nickel for every time an older mom offered the sage advice to, "Enjoy your children—it goes by in a blink," I'd be a wealthy woman. I couldn't comprehend the "blink" part when time seemed to crawl during the exhausting preschool chapter of motherhood. When my kids were young and dependent on me in every area of their lives, I couldn't imagine a day when I would no longer change a diaper, pack a diaper bag, schedule my errands around nap times, or awaken in the middle of the night to a tiny sniffle heard on a baby monitor. But that moment did arrive. And the next one and the next. The clock kept ticking, and eventually I became the mother who told mothers with younger children that it all goes by in a blink.

Hindrances to Letting Go

When it comes to letting go, many mothers have a hard time loosening their grip, and they fall prey to being over-protective. I'm certainly not endorsing a parenting philosophy that advocates foregoing the outlet protectors and chucking the bike helmets. I'm talking about over-the-top, extreme overprotection. The kind of parenting where you might forbid your child from engaging in activities that most other children their age are allowed to experience. Are you the mom who goes through a religious ritual of slathering your child in hand sanitizer before (and after) he hits the playscape at the park? Or the mother who won't allow your child to play most any sport because it might be dangerous? Or maybe the mother whose child has rarely been left with a family member or baby-sitter because you have a hard time pulling away?

Another common hindrance to letting go is rescuing children from the consequences of their actions. Are you the mother who rushes up to the school to deliver your child's forgotten lunch, homework assignment, or team jersey on game day? (Busted, busted, and busted again.) Once or twice is understandable, but if this is a habit, bailing your child out does more harm in the long run. How will they ever learn the importance of remembering their backpacks if you always have their backs? Perhaps you are the mom who calls the school, coach, or teacher to find out why your child didn't get the homeroom teacher you requested, why she didn't make the A team, or why he scored poorly on a class project. When your child leaves the nest and enters college or the workforce, try contacting his boss or college dean to get some answers and let me know how that works out for you! Or better yet, let me know how that benefited your child. As painful as it may be, we must allow our children to experience consequences related to poor choices they make. They must learn how to deal with life's injustices. The real world will not coddle them, console them, protect them, or rescue them. Nor should we.

Loosening the Grip

Ecclesiastes 3:6 reminds us there is "a right time to hold on and another to let go" (*The Message*). Obviously, we hold on tight to our children in the early years when they are dependent on us for their protection and well-being. By the time our children leave the nest, we need to know how to let go physically, emotionally, and even spiritually. In order to do that, we must learn to let go gradually as they progress from infant to young adult. It's easier said than done. And it can be painful.

I recall a time a few years back when my daughter was attending college out of state. She had been having some side effects to a medication the dermatologist in town had prescribed to her, so I insisted she make an appointment to address the problem. In the meantime, I researched possible drug alternatives online and found a possible alternative. I texted my daughter the name of the drug and told her to ask the doctor about it. While she was in the appointment, I texted her to see what the doctor recommended (yes, I am well aware that every step in this process qualifies me for helicopter-mom-of-the-year). She replied back that she was still in the appointment but that the doctor had recommended a different drug. A drug, mind you, that I had read about in my five minutes of extensive online research that was known to have a vast array of side effects.

At this point, I did what any concerned mother of a nineteen-year-old would do. I picked up my phone and called my child while she was in the appointment. When she answered, I asked to speak to the dermatologist. She obediently handed over the phone to the doctor, and I politely expressed my concerns about the drug she had prescribed. There was a long pause, and then she politely informed me that before she could address my concerns, she would need to get my daughter's permission to discuss her medical records with me, since my daughter was a legal adult. Excuse me?! She's a baby, for heaven's sake! I'm her MOTHER. When I hung up the phone, I felt rather foolish, but I also felt a twinge of sadness over the reminder that it was time to let go. In truth, my daughter could have handled the situation on her own.

Now, with two children married, I've improved somewhat and certainly don't meddle in their lives. However, my youngest is in college, and I've had a hard time letting go when it comes to worrying about his safety. I recently got on Facebook and saw a picture of my college-age son in my newsfeed, and it launched me into full-fledged panic mode. My son loves hiking and being outdoors, so we had bought him a portable hammock with two end-straps that can be hung pretty much anywhere where trees can be found. Of course, I imagined he would use the hammock at campgrounds or along hiking trails—not hanging high above a creek bed latched to a steep cliff side! Let's just say that at that moment I failed miserably when it came to the "letting go" part.

I immediately lit up his phone with text messages and phone calls to let him know exactly how I felt about his latest adventure. Included in the messages was a reminder that the frontal lobe of the boy brain (where actions are connected to consequences) is not fully developed until the mid-late twenties. I further reminded him that God has appointed me to be his frontal lobe in the interim to ward off dumb choices, like hanging hammocks from steep hillsides. All I got in return was a simple, "haha mom. whatever."

Bigger Hands than Ours

Learning to let go has been one of the hardest challenges I've faced as a mother. Our nature as moms is to hold on, protect, nurture, and rescue. We are hardwired to rush to them when they fall down, check on them in the middle of the night to make they have enough bedcovers, wonder if they have friends to sit by at lunch on their first day of school (and every day thereafter), and worry about their ability to get into college someday (this anxiety begins when they enter preschool). The mental list of worries regarding our children is endless. However, when we loosen our grip, we are able to gently take their hand out of our own and place it directly into the hand of God.

God's plan is that we prepare our children to someday leave. We are to be in the process of letting go while they remain in our nests, rather than hold tight to the last possible second. Moms who have based their entire identity on being a mother will struggle with this concept. It's hard for them to imagine a day will come when they won't be clocking in daily as a mother. This is why it's important for moms to keep the flame alive in their marriages, as well as develop outside interests other than the children. Keep up with and nurture your friendships. Plan a girl's weekend trip with your best girl-friends and make it an annual thing. Find hobbies that aren't tied to your children. Step out of your normal comfort zone. Take up a challenging project or learn a new skill. Go back to work or consider starting a home-based business. Join a gym or take up running. If you haven't found your place in ministry, volunteer at your church or for a local ministry.

You are more than a Mrs. and more than a mom, so don't tie your primary identity to being a wife and mother—that place belongs to your relationship with Christ. In his book *Counterfeit Gods*, author Timothy Keller says, "If we look to some created thing to give us the meaning, hope, and happiness that only God himself can give, it will eventually fail to deliver and break our hearts."[1] God never intended that our children be at the center of our worship. Mothers who put Christ at the center of their lives may experience sadness when their last child leaves the nest, but they will not be derailed. As mothers, our calling is to hold on loosely and point our children to the one who will never loosen his grip. ❧

Notes

1. Timothy Keller, *Counterfeit Gods* (New York: Penguin Group, 2009), 3.

Chapter 14

I Love Me; I Love Me Not

I recently stumbled upon a picture of my pregnant self taken just days shy of delivering my first child. How this photo survived the shredder is beyond me. I had gained a whopping sixty-eight pounds and looked like one of the Oompa-Loompas from *Willy Wonka and the Chocolate Factory*. Honestly, I have no good excuse for gaining sixty-eight pounds in my first pregnancy, other than a mysterious craving for just about everything on the menu at Taco Bell. And it certainly didn't help matters when I was ordered to bed rest at the thirty-week mark due to early labor. What's a girl to do? Eat more Taco Bell, I tell you. While my husband and I laugh about my weight gain during the first pregnancy (and second . . . and third), it was anything but funny at the time. I remember being panicked that I would never be able to get the weight off, but I was obviously not panicked enough to put down the Cheesy Gordito Crunch. For the record, the weight did come off pretty fast (at least after the first pregnancy), and I was able once again to make momentary peace in the never-ending body wars.

However, that peace was always fleeting. It was easily interrupted by any number of triggers waiting just around the corner. It could be a higher-than-expected number on a scale. Or a tug-of-war in the dressing room while trying on a pair of jeans. Or two minutes of swimsuit shopping. It could be a simple glance into the mirror after getting out of the shower. I know I'm not alone when it comes to the love-hate relationship (or for many of us, the loathe-hate relationship) we women have when seeing our reflections in the mirror. One study found that 93 percent of girls and young women report feeling anxiety or stress about some aspect of their looks when getting ready in the morning.[1] In this chapter, we are going to address the appearance battle that has waged war in many of our souls and has caused an endless amount of grief among women. Better yet, we are going to discuss tangible ways we can make peace with our reflections and define beauty according to God's standards rather than the culture's narrow standards.

Peace, Love, and Body Wars

As someone who struggled in the past with an eating disorder (high school, college, and young thirties), I am far from an expert on the topic of body image. However, I have come a long way in learning to "make friends with my body." My focus today is on looking healthy rather than stepping on the scale and allowing the number I see to dictate my mood for the day. The truth is, most women hate their bodies. And why wouldn't we? We are bombarded with images (most airbrushed, I'm sure) of perfect bodies and told the standard is "the smaller the better." In addition, most of us were never warned that our body shape would change as we got older and especially after we have children. In our ignorance, we hold fast to this image of our fifteen- to eighteen-year-old toned selves and forever make it the standard. To add to this pressure, culture's standard of beauty does not allow for the natural effects of child-bearing or aging. Culture's definition of beauty does not tolerate stretch marks, cellulite, or muffin-top bellies.

To add further insult to injury, we are assaulted in the supermarket checkout lines by magazines covers with celebrity moms holding their newborns and showing off their postbaby bods. The magazines promise to tout the celebrity mom's secrets to her "air-brushed" figure on the inside pages and leave us believing we, too, can look just like them. Of course, they fail to leave out the real secrets, which amount to: personal chefs, personal trainers, nannies to watch their babies while they work out, and a clause in their contracts stating that they have final approval on all cover images before they go to print. (Translation: The images will undergo the Photoshop knife before they land in that supermarket rack.)

It's not just the celebrity moms taunting us from the magazine covers. Just about every image we see of a celebrity has been airbrushed to oblivion and back. Yet, how many of us have aspired to the images we see? Or at the very least, sighed heavily when we run across them? Let me put it into perspective for you: The celebrities themselves are sighing when they see the images and wishing they could look like the airbrushed versions of themselves!

Another area that contributes or our personal body wars is a failure to accept our God-given body shapes. If you've ever grumbled in the dressing room while shopping because the clothes never seem to flatter your shape, you are not alone. The majority of clothes made today are made to fit the least common body shape among women. A study found that the hourglass figure is the least dominant shape of women, making up only 8 percent of the 6,318 U.S. women that were scanned for the study. The study further found that the hourglass shape almost does not exist in women larger than a size eight.[2] Keep in mind that the average woman is 5' 3.8" and weighs 163 pounds.[3] The same study found that the garment industry assumes that the hourglass figure is the dominant shape of American women and designs their clothing accordingly. In fact, 46 percent of women were found to have more of a rectangle shape, 21 percent were spoon shaped, and 14 percent were shaped more like an inverted triangle.[4]

Add the problem of cellulite to the list of body woes. Again, most of us don't know that cellulite is present in approximately 85 percent of women and typically begins in adolescence when the body begins to produce the female hormone estrogen.[5] It is normal to have cellulite. It is not linked to being overweight. Skinny people have cellulite. Young people have cellulite. Celebrities have cellulite, and even supermodels have cellulite. Regardless, it is still labeled as a flaw that results from our negligence. Many women continue to buy into the common myth that cellulite can be improved (or removed completely) by diet, exercise, and drinking more water.[6] This is simply not true. Having cellulite is part of being a woman, so think twice before buying that cream that keeps popping up in the right-hand margin of your Facebook page. Chances are, it's a scam.

There is absolutely nothing wrong with wanting to improve our appearance and/or our bodies, but we need to make sure we haven't set unrealistic goals that will leave us disappointed in the end. We need to make the best of what God has given us and stop comparing ourselves to the best features we see in others. One of my biggest regrets is the amount of time I have spent grumbling and complaining about my body, complexion, cellulite, thighs, etc., in a futile attempt to fit the culture's standard for an ideal body. I wasted valuable time obsessing over vanity when my focus should have been the pursuit of the timeless qualities of virtue and investing in a brand of beauty that never fades over time.

Vintage Beauty Secrets

In my book, *5 Conversations You Must Have with Your Daughter*, I shared how women's attitudes about beauty and body image have changed over the past century. I referenced a book called *The Body Project* by author Joan Jacobs Brumberg, who researched girls' diaries and journals from the late 1800s to early 1900s to track the shift in attitudes regarding appearance. The results of her research helped shed some light on how beauty moved from an internal focus to an external focus over the years. Brumberg found that "Before World War I, girls rarely mentioned their bodies in terms of strategies for self-improvement or struggles for personal identity." She states:

> When girls in the nineteenth century thought about ways to improve themselves, they almost always focused on their internal character and how it was reflected in outward behavior. In 1882, the personal agenda of an adolescent diarist read: "Resolved, not to talk about myself or feelings. To think before speaking. To work seriously. To be self restrained in conversation and actions. Not to let my thoughts wander. To be dignified. Interest myself more in others."[7]

Can you imagine opening up your daughter's diary and reading "Dear Diary, help me to be pretty on the inside." That's what a mother in the late 1800s might be likely to find. And it's most certainly what mothers in the 1800s were modeling to their daughters. Brumberg notes that girls from the nineteenth century were discouraged from showing too much attention to appearance—to do so would be vanity. The book notes that "character was built on attention to self-control, service to others, and belief in God."[8] Clearly, girls and their mothers were looking to God's Word to define the standard for beauty. Proverbs 31:30 was no doubt, their standard: "Charm is deceptive, and beauty is fleeting; but a woman who fears the LORD is to be praised" (NIV).

Brumberg notes several key factors that influenced a standard of beauty rooted in godly character. First of all, there were no premanufactured sizes during this time. Brumberg says:

> In general, mass-produced clothing fostered autonomy in girls because it took matters of style and taste outside the dominion of the mother, who had traditionally made and supervised a girl's wardrobe. . . . So long as clothing was made at home, the dimensions of the garment could be adjusted to the particular body intended to wear it. But with store-bought clothes, the body had to fit instantaneously into standard sizes that were constructed from a pattern representing a norm. When clothing failed to fit the body,

particularly a part as intimate as the breasts, young women were apt to perceive that there was something wrong with their bodies.[9]

Now, I'm certainly not suggesting we brush the dust off our old Singer sewing machines and take to making our own wardrobes. Given my elementary sewing skills, I would be forced to settle for those simple pillowcase dresses you often see on toddler girls. Matching hair bow optional.

Brumberg also notes that bathroom mirrors were not the norm in homes until the end of the nineteenth century. She states:

> When the mirror became a staple of the American middle-class home at the end of the nineteenth century, attention to adolescent acne escalated, as did sales of products for the face. Until then, pimples were primarily a tactile experience, at least for the girl who had them. But that all changed in the late 1800s with the widespread adoption in middle-class homes of a bathroom sink with running water and a mirror hung above it.[10]

She further notes that, "mirrors play a critical role in the way American girls have assessed their own faces and figures."[11] As mirrors became popularized, women were able to scrutinize and compare their features with the women they saw in movies and magazines, not to mention each other.

In the 1920s, American women also began to interest in cosmetics. From facial powders to rouge, lipstick, and even eyelash curlers, women flocked to the local drugstores to stock up on these beauty accoutrements. The "flapper movement" further boosted sales of cosmetics among women. Brumberg notes that "sales of compacts (small handheld mirrors with a compartment for powder) soared because they allowed women to scrutinize and 'reconstruct' the face almost anywhere, in a moment's notice."[12] Shortly thereafter, home scales became available and managing weight became a preoccupation among young women. Until then, the only place a young woman could weigh herself was the drugstore or county fair. (Nothing like weighing yourself after a day's worth of corn dogs and funnel cakes!) Prior to that, dieting and exercise were virtually unheard of and, again, would have been considered a measure of vanity.

I was shocked to discover in Brumberg's book that when young women in the late 1800s left home, they would often write their mothers and speak of healthy weight gain and voracious eating habits. It was considered a curse to be slender! Slender girls were thought to be unhealthy and subject to worries of infertility. The ability to bear healthy children was of far greater importance than looking svelte in a swimsuit. As mirrors became more prevalent and the flapper movement gained momentum in the 1920s, women began to express worry over gaining weight, and, soon after, "dieting" or "food restriction" became a common topic. The shift from virtue to vanity has been a runaway train ever since.

I think it's important we overview the time line of women's attitudes regarding a standard for beauty so that we can better understand how we got to where we are today. It's hard to imagine that a time existed in such relatively recent history when virtue was considered beauty and vanity was considered sin. A time when women didn't check their reflections in a mirror multiple times throughout the day to critique every square inch of their faces and bodies. A time when they didn't obsess over signs of aging or the latest fad diet. A time when they didn't weigh daily (or multiple times a day) and allow the number on the scale to dictate their mood for the remainder of the day. A time when they didn't compare their dress size to their girlfriends' dress sizes. While it might not be possible to do away with mirrors, scales, and makeup, there are few things we can learn from our sisters of ages past.

First, we can commit to check our reflections less throughout the day. Second, we can pull away when we begin to lapse into a tailspin of grief over the things we want to tweak, lose, enhance, nip, or tuck. Third, we can also commit to get on the scales less and focus more on exercise and nutrition. Fourth, we can refuse to throw dressing room pity parties when the sizes we grab fit more snugly than they used to. Most importantly, we can commit to turn our primary focus to godly character rather than worldly appearance. It's time to redefine beauty.

Beauty Redefined

I ran across a heartbreaking statistic recently that left me further burdened to see a new movement where beauty is redefined. A study commissioned by the Dove Foundation found that only 2 percent of women would describe themselves as beautiful.[13] Are you included in that small sampling? If I had a mission statement for this chapter, it would be to see that percentage go up and your names added to the sampling of women who consider themselves beautiful. The study further found that 57 percent of all women strongly agree that "the attributes of female beauty have become very narrowly defined in today's world," and 68 percent strongly agree that "the media and advertising set an unrealistic standard of beauty that most women can't ever achieve."[14]

The challenge to redefine beauty is nothing new. God cautioned his people long ago against judging a person based on the sum of their external parts. When the prophet Samuel was called by God to anoint the next king to follow Saul, God chastised him for assuming that David's older brother, Eliab, might be next in line to the throne based on his handsome appearance. In 1 Samuel 16:6, Samuel took one look at Eliab and thought, "Surely the LORD's anointed stands here before the LORD" (NIV). The verse that follows reveals God's standard for judging beauty when he tells Samuel, "Do not consider his appearance or his height, for I have rejected him. The LORD does not look at the things man looks at. Man looks at the outward appearance, but the Lord looks at the heart" (1 Sam. 16:7 NIV).

Isn't that a comforting thought? While the rest of the world may judge us for what they see on the outside, God judges us for what he sees on the inside. Beauty is not defined by a number on the scale, a premanufactured clothing size, an hourglass body shape, washboard abs, slender thighs, the latest name-brand fashion, a cleavage-baring top, a new sassy haircut, a clear complexion, an antiwrinkle cream, or a surgical procedure. While some of the above may garner the world's approval, they don't impress God in the least.

It will not be possible to readjust our attitudes regarding beauty unless we first come to a place where we are more concerned with the condition of our hearts than the temporary shells that house them. Stop for a minute and calculate (roughly) about how much time and attention you spend each day beautifying the outer shell that houses your heart. What if we were to reverse that formula? What if we began to worry more about correcting true flaws that exist beneath the surface of our outward appearance? The most beautiful women have discovered this beauty secret. Are you one of them?

At the beginning of this chapter, I mentioned that this topic is near and dear to my heart because I have struggled over the years to base my worth on who I am on the inside rather than what I look like on the outside. It is a constant battle for me, and some days I walk away a winner. Other days, not so much. This chapter is as much for me as it is for you. If you have also bought into the culture's lies regarding beauty, it will take time to readjust your attitude and conform to God's standard. You will have to ask for God's grace and help when you lapse into your old ways and actively (even when you don't feel like it) replace the lies with God's amazing truths.

Just this past week, I woke up with the most unsightly blemish on my face—no doubt a result of stress (book deadline, hello!) and failing to pack my regular face cleanser for the past two out-of-town weekend events. I had no choice but to use the commercial grade hotel soap bar, and the result was this darling blemish. Let me confess to you right now that there was no amount of hearty laughter over the timing of this blemish when I spotted it in the mirror. There was sheer disgust. Further scrutiny. Brief consideration of canceling a coffee date with a friend scheduled later in the day. Doctoring the blemish. More scrutiny. Mental calculations of how many days it may take for it to go away. Panic that it may stick around for my upcoming weekend event.

This downward spiral resulted in an all-too-familiar pity party over my troublesome complexion. I mean, really. How many women pushing fifty are still having acne breakouts? At what point am I done with puberty?! I may or may not have even asked those questions out loud to God. Again. For the bazillionith time. It's embarrassing enough to sit in a dermatologist's waiting room with a dozen or more teenagers. I wonder if I can get a senior citizen discount on that Proactiv stuff all the celebrity teenagers are touting. Ah, but I digress. Back to the mirror for more scrutiny. (Heavy sighing ensues.) Was it my imagination, or had it grown bigger since I last looked? I mumbled something to myself about there being no amount of cover-up to hide this unwelcome intruder. After doctoring it up some more, I went downstairs and began to write this chapter. I may have even taken a short break to Google "how to get rid of blemish the size of Mount Rushmore." And then I returned to writing this chapter. At some point along the way as I continued typing God's truths into this chapter for YOUR benefit, I realized the irony of the timing of this unsightly blemish. And I had to laugh. I even took a minute to thank God for using the blemish to remind me (yet again) that true beauty resides in the heart. And I may or may not have also thanked him for my tube of Clinique Advanced Concealer, which I will no doubt go through by the end of the weekend.

For the record, the blemish was still front and center for my weekend event in spite of the cover-up. I wrestled with my insecurities as my plane descended, knowing the pastor's wife was meeting me at the airport to transport me to the venue. I had worked myself up to the point that I imagined she might run away, shrieking in terror when she saw me. Once again, I had to take a deep breath and remind myself of God's truths regarding beauty and self-worth. After grabbing my bags from the baggage carousel, I headed outside to meet my designated ride. When the pastor's wife got out of her car, I couldn't believe it. She had two small round Band-Aids on her face! She immediately began to explain that she had just had two sun-damaged areas removed and had stressed over having to meet me with her face all patched up. Does our God have a sense of humor, or what? I told her my story, and we both laughed at the irony. Clearly, God had a lesson for us both in the midst of the irony.

I'm in the battle with you as we learn to love ourselves and see ourselves through God's lens rather than the lens of the world. Will you join me in starting a movement to redefine beauty? Let's not waste another minute allowing the blemishes, wrinkles, spider veins, extra pounds, gray hairs, sagging body parts, or _____ (you fill in the blank with your own body woes) to distract us from seeing and loving the beautiful person God created each of us to be. True beauty resides in the heart. Invest your time in the only beauty secret that will stand the test of time. You have my guarantee that it will work. Tell you what: Try it for thirty days, and if you're not completely satisfied, you can have your vanity back.

Notes

1. Anastasia Goodstein, "What Can Industry Do to Stop the Onslaught?" *The Huffington Post*, posted October 2, 2007, http://www.huffingtonpost.com/anastasia-goodstein/what-can-industry-do-to-s_b_66798.html.

2. "Fashion Designers Still Blind to Reality," February 23, 2006, http://www.aphroditewomenshealth.com/news/20060123003254_health_news.shtml.

3. See http://pediatrics.about.com/cs/growthcharts2/f/avg_ht_female.htm.

4. "Fashion Designers Still Blind to Reality," February 23, 2006.

5. See http://beauty.ivillage.com/skinbody/cellulite/0,,newbeauty_8ht9nz4l,00.html; http://www.vanguardngr.com/articles/2002/features/fashion/fas223072006.html.

6. Ibid.

7. Joan Jacobs Brumberg, *The Body Project: An Intimate History of American Girls* (New York: Vintage Books, 1998), xxi.

8. Ibid., xx.

9. Ibid., 107.

10. Ibid., 64

11. Ibid.

12. Ibid., 68.

13. "New Global Study Uncovers Desire for Broader Definition of Beauty," *New York*, September 29, 2004, http://www.campaignforreal-beauty.com/press.asp?section=news&id=110.

14. Ibid.

Chapter 15

Fine Whines: Aged to Perfection

*T*ime, wrote Milton, is "the subtle thief of youth."[1] I was reminded of that tidbit of wisdom on a recent afternoon while walking through the mall with my daughter. While en route to our target destination, our mission was suddenly interrupted by a chirpy mall kiosk employee with an overzealous sales pitch to "come try my antiaging eye cream, pretty ladies." And by "we," I'm pretty sure she meant "me," since my daughter is all of twenty-two years old and is often mistaken for a high-schooler. Look, it's hard enough to grow old behind closed doors, but do we have to address my crow's-feet and laugh lines in the middle of the mall? Sorry, kiosk lady, but I'm not taking the bait even if you did attach "pretty ladies" onto your sales pitch in a desperate attempt to score a sale. When we walked by, I gave little Miss Chirpy my best daggers glance which, now that I think about it, probably accentuated my eye wrinkles even more. Sigh.

It's bad enough that every time I log onto Facebook, I'm heckled by the margin ads that are targeted to the aging Baby Boomer demographic. Thanks to giving Facebook my date of birth at some point in the sign-up process, I have now been classified in the category of panicked women in a desperate search for the fountain of youth. And I'm not sure if Facebook has been going through my lake photos, but they have also determined I'm a good candidate for some Acai berry potion that will melt away my muffin top in fourteen days. Bug off, Facebook. Unless of course, that Acai berry potion really works, and then yeah, send me a sample. Just recently, Facebook has taken it to a whole new level and begun targeting me with laser liposuction ads for $1,249 per session (per body part) as well as an assisted living care plan. I haven't even qualified for a senior citizen discount yet, and Facebook is ready to lock me up in an assisted care facility. Unless it is at a five-star resort with a world-renowned chef whipping up my fiber-friendly meals while I lounge by the poolside wearing one of those skirted swim-dresses I swore I'd never buy, count me out. What's next, casket and tombstone ads?

As if I need the aging reminders. All I have to do is look in the mirror to see that my "I just woke up face" of my younger years has become my "everyday face" of my current years. I am one click away from trying the next Botox offer that lands in my Inbox from Groupon. Oh, I kid. For now, at least. Between the wrinkles, spider veins, spirally gray hairs, and inability to see text without a pair of reading glasses, I don't need any additional reminders that I'm on the threshold of turning fifty. And don't even get me started on the delightful perimenopausal symptoms that literally came out of nowhere and left me wanting to move to the tundra and rip the heads off small, innocent kittens—or my husband, since we don't own a kitten and he is more handy to drag along on my emotional roller coasters.

Probably my biggest adjustment to date has been the inability to read the text on a label, clothing tag, or incoming text message without locating a pair of reading glasses. If I forget them, I'm toast. This has caused few mishaps when texting my children and provided them with endless amounts of entertainment at my expense. In fact, my youngest son recently posted the screenshot on the next page of a text conversation we had on his Facebook wall. (File this under "reasons parents shouldn't text.")

```
·ıl.... Verizon 🤏        11:43 AM           ▭
  Messages         Hayden          Edit
              Feb 14, 2012 11:27 AM

  Happy valentines day to
  the most important woman
  in my life! 😍 😘 🤍 💘
  love you momma

              That is so sweet. I'm
              saving this message
              forevs. Does this mean
              you're willing to go on a
              mommy daughter date in
              our new matching
              outfits?!!

  Mom this is Hayden. What
  the heck?

  Are you ok?
```

No, son, I'm not OK. I wasn't wearing my glasses, and therefore I thought the message you sent was from your sister, Paige, because "Paige" and "Hayden" look just the same to me without my reading glasses. But I have recently stumbled upon some ammo for when my kids taunt me about getting old. Consider this interesting bit of information regarding the aging process. If you're young, read it and weep. If you're old and your kids are kind enough to remind you of that fact on a regular basis, read it to your children and watch them weep. According to an article on CNN.com, there are six stages of life: infancy, childhood, adolescence, young adulthood, middle adulthood, and senior adulthood.

The description of "Young Adulthood" is what caught me by surprise. Here is what it says:

A person reaches physical maturity and stops growing around age 18. As early as age 20, people may notice the beginning signs of aging; fine wrinkles, thinning skin, loss of firmness in hands and neck, graying hair, hair loss and thinning nails. At age 30, the human body's major organs begin to decline.[2]

You can bet I have read that paragraph out loud countless times to my "aging" children. In fact, my older two children are in their young twenties, and I remind them often that they are just a few years shy of thirty when their major organs begin to shut down. Maybe "shut down" is a bit extreme, but it certainly gets the point across.

The Fine Line on Wrinkles

Growing old gracefully has never been more difficult than in today's culture. Everywhere we turn, we are reminded of our flaws and bombarded with countless solutions (most costing big bucks) to fix these flaws. Shave off ten years! Look younger! Antiaging scams have become a multibillion-dollar industry. One market research firm predicts that the Boomer demographic alone "will push the U.S. market for antiaging products from about $80 billion (in 2011) to more than $114 billion by 2015."[3] We are lining up at the fountain of youth like a herd of gullible junkies looking for the latest and greatest anti-aging fix.

Women aren't the only ones chasing the antiaging trend. From scalp stimulants and hair revitalizers to eye creams and alpha-hydroxy peels, some men have become as vain as their female counterparts. And don't even get me started on the erectile dysfunction commercials that feature the couple in the side-by-side outdoor bathtubs. Someone, please make them go away. But whatever you do, don't let the camera follow them to wherever they go!

This antiaging trend has become so prevalent that the National Institute on Aging recently weighed in and cautioned consumers to be skeptical when it comes to antiaging claims made by products and services. "Our culture places great value on staying young, but aging is normal," the Institute says. They further say, "Despite claims about pills or treatments that lead to endless youth, no treatments have been proven to slow or reverse the aging process."[4] They offered basic advice for aging well, which amounted to a healthy diet, regular exercise, and not smoking. Duh. Like we didn't know that already.

S. Jay Olshansky, a professor at the University of Illinois-Chicago's School of Public Health who has written extensively about aging, advises that "if someone is promising you today that you can slow, stop or reverse aging, they're likely trying hard to separate you from your money."[5] Naomi Wolf, author of *The Beauty Myth*, says, "Magazines, consciously or half-consciously, must project the attitude that looking one's age is bad because $650 million of their ad revenue comes from people who would go out of business if visible age looked good."[6] Despite these warnings, many of us will continue to take the bait.

If we could truly reverse the hands of time, wouldn't we be seeing some tangible, convincing evidence by now? For example, take facial serums. *Consumer Reports* has begun including antiaging cosmetics in their reviews and tested nine face serums, all available at drug stores for prices ranging from $20 to $65, and all of which claimed to reduce wrinkles. To test the accuracy of the manufacturer's claims, *Consumer Reports* used high-tech optical devices and other scientific methods to assess the products. They found that "after six weeks of use, the effectiveness of even the best products was limited and varied from subject to subject."[7] They further reported that "when we did see wrinkle reductions, they were at best slight, and they fell short of the miracles that manufacturers seemed to imply on product labels."[8] I wonder how many women would be willing to continue pumping their money into a product that at best would only deliver "slight" improvement? Maybe my grandmother's nighttime ritual of slathering on Pond's Beauty Cream from the local drugstore is the way to go after all.

Consumer Reports also tested wrinkle creams and reported that "even the best performers reduced the average depth of wrinkles by less than 10 percent, a magnitude of change that was, alas, barely visible to the naked eye." (As an interesting side-note, the top-rated product was one that cost about $19 at the time of the testing. The most expensive, which costs a whopping $335, was rated among the least effective.) They also tested sixteen over-the-counter eye creams and reported that "even among the best-performing products, wrinkle reduction around the eyes was generally pretty subtle. . . . After six weeks of daily use, none came close to eliminating wrinkles."[9]

I'm not picking on you if you've jumped on the culture's antiaging bandwagon. I have a tube of one of these rescuers in my bathroom drawer along with a few other (OK, a dozen or so) facial serums and wrinkle creams I have purchased over the years. Fortunately I didn't shell out $335 for any of them, but had someone convinced me it was the fountain of youth in a bottle, and backed the claim up with before-and-after (airbrushed, *cough, cough*) pictures as further evidence, I'd probably be back to hiding it in the back of my closet until the credit card bill comes. Trust me, this chapter is written just as much (or more) for me than anyone else. When it comes to aging gracefully, I have a long way to go. My goal is not to interrupt your beauty routine, unless of course, it needs to be interrupted. So much of what we are told are flaws that need to be eliminated, corrected, erased, or softened are viewed by God as marks of beauty as we mature in both age and wisdom. Maybe our biggest flaw is that we have believed the culture's lie when it comes to aging.

Pro-Aging

When I was a young adult, I remember thinking forty was so old and fifty, well, that was one foot in the grave! Yet the closer I got to forty, the less old I thought it was old. As I quickly approach my fiftieth birthday, I feel the same way. "Inside every older person is a younger person wondering what happened."[10] So very true.

I keep hearing, "fifty is the new forty" and "forty is the new thirty." But what's wrong with fifty being fifty, forty being forty, and thirty being thirty? I, for one, have absolutely no desire to go back to my thirties and relearn some of the hard lessons that have contributed to who I am today. No thank you. Every season of life comes with both benefits and challenges. Proverbs 20:29 reminds us, "The glory of young men is their strength, but the splendor of old men is their gray hair" (ESV). The New Living Translation adds, "the gray hair of experience is the splendor of the old." One Bible commentary notes, "In Hebrew culture the young and the old each had a particular excellence not possessed by the other. The young took pride in their physical strength, the older in their wisdom, revealed by their gray hair."[11] Obviously, the point is not having gray hair, but rather that those who are older are typically those to have gray hair—but more importantly, experience and wisdom.

When I find myself grumbling over a new spider vein cropping up on my legs, a more pronounced wrinkle on my face, or yet another hot flash (and you thought PMS was fun!), I stop and remind myself that I have something my younger friends will have to earn over time—experience and wisdom. They can have their wonderfully toned arms, eyes that can see, and menstrual cycles, but I choose to be grateful for what I have (unless these hot flashes get too bad, and then I might consider making a trade). Oliver Wendell Holmes Jr. once said, "To be 70 years young is sometimes far more cheerful and hopeful than to be 40 years old."[12] Amen to that.

If reversing the signs of aging has become a greater priority than progressing the signs of inner beauty, then it's time to reorder our priorities. Are we more attentive to correcting perceived flaws on the outside or correcting the true flaws that reside in our hearts? Do we spend more time, money, and energy improving the outside of the temple or the inside of the temple? Or for that matter, do we spend more time investing in the kingdom or our antiaging efforts? Do we find ourselves longing more for compliments related to our outer appearance or our inner beauty? When our time is up and our friends and family members parade past our coffins, do we hope to hear, "Wow, doesn't she look great," Or, "Wow, what a beautiful, godly woman she was!"? No amount of wrinkle creams, Botox, or plastic surgery will be able to stop the hands of time. At the end of the day, we're still the number of years on our driver's licenses, and nothing will change that fact. Some day we will shed these aging, earthly tents and leave this vain-stricken world behind.

Too often, our years are spent longing for the days of past. Life isn't over when your body begins to grow old, so make sure your primary identity is not wrapped up in being or looking young. Life isn't over when the last child leaves the nest, so make sure your primary identity isn't wrapped up in being a mother. Life isn't over when you retire from your job, so make sure your primary identity is not wrapped up in your job. Life isn't over when the awards and accolades begin to taper off, so make sure your primary identity is not wrapped up in your performance. Life isn't over should you lose your job or savings, so make sure your primary identity is not wrapped up in money. Life isn't over if your marriage fails or your husband retires to heaven before you, so make sure your primary identity is not wrapped up in being a wife. No doubt, some of these things can bring us great joy during the courses of our lives, but they were never meant to define us or become our primary identity.

On that day when we stand before God face-to-face, we will not come with résumés touting our status as workers, servants, friends, wives, or mothers. We will not haul our trophies, possessions, awards, money, or homes behind us. We will not stand hand-in-hand with our loved ones and present ourselves as part of a collective whole. And we will not arrive dressed fashionably, accessorized, and looking ten years younger. We will face God based on our identity in Christ and Christ alone. Invest every chapter of your life with that moment in sight, and you can't help but age gracefully. ～♨

Notes

1. John Milton (December 9, 1608–November 8, 1674), http://quotationsbook.com/quote/1624/.

2. CNN.com, "Effects of aging on your body," http://www.cnn.com/2007/HEALTH/07/27/life.stages/index.htm, August 14, 2007.

3. Davus Crary, "Boomers Will Be Pumping Billions iInto Anti-Aging Industry," August 20, 2011, http://www.huffingtonpost.com/2011/08/20/boomers-anti-aging-industry_n_932109.html.

4. See http://www.webmd.com/healthy-beauty/news/20040813/spotting-anti-aging-scams.

5. Ibid.

6. Naomi Wolf, *The Beauty Myth: How Images of Beauty Are Used Against Women* (New York: Harper Collins, 2002), 84. **Note:** I do not endorse this book as a whole and disagree wholeheartedly with the author's radical feminist view and negative view of Christianity but found some of the research to be useful in citing the media's damage when it comes to the "beauty myth."

7. See http://www.huffingtonpost.com/2011/08/20/boomers-anti-aging-industry_n_932109.html.

8. Ibid.

9. Ibid.

10. Jennifer Yane, http://en.wikiquote.org/wiki/Growing_old.

11. J. F. Walvoord, R. B. Zuck, and Dallas Theological Seminary, *The Bible Knowledge Commentary: An Exposition of the Scriptures* (Wheaton, IL: Victor Books, 1983), Proverbs 20:29.

12. Oliver Wendell Holmes Jr., http://thinkexist.com/quotation/to_be-years_young_is_sometimes_far_more_cheerful/148880.html.

Chapter 16

Happily-Ever-After

If you happen to read fairy tales, you will observe that one idea runs from one end of them to the other—the idea that peace and happiness can only exist on some condition. This idea, which is the core of ethics, is the core of the nursery-tales.

~G. K. CHESTERTON

Happiness. We yearn for it. It becomes the dangling carrot we chase throughout our lives. Most every product or service is marketed to appeal to our deep desire to find happiness. Like addicts, we hop from one buzz to another, seduced by promises that the carrot we are chasing will deliver peace to our souls. If we can catch it. Buy it. Consume it. Wear it. Even if the peace only lasts for a moment—one moment where we can feel like everything is right in the world. Once gone, the chase is on again. The carrot of happiness dangles ever before us but, somehow, just out of our grasp. If only we could find the secret to spending more of our time in the present moment rather than in the chase. Even if we never catch the carrots we chase.

I remember a conversation I had years ago with a fellow mom whose children attended school with my children. Truth be told, I was jealous of this mom. She had cute clothes. She jetted off to fancy places with her husband. Drove a cool SUV with all the fancy upgrades. She lived in a house that looked like it belonged on the cover of *Southern Living*. Her children were well-behaved and said "yes ma'am" and "no ma'am." And as if that wasn't enough, she was a teeny size two. She had a lot of carrots. All at the same time. While the rest of us were engaged in the dangling carrot chase, I imagined her sitting by the poolside at the country club, sipping on one of those fancy umbrella drinks. *She must be so happy*, I thought. Her biggest worry of the day probably boiled down to whether or not she could fit in a game of tennis before carpool duty beckoned.

I'm sure it was by no accident that soon after that thought, God allowed one of those divine appointments in which my life would intersect with hers. We were working on a volunteer activity for the school and, somehow, the topic of raising kids came up. "I just want my children to grow up and be happy," she said. "I never feel like it's enough. I know happiness can't be bought, but their focus always seems to be on the next cool trend or gadget or activity that their friends are engaged in. Honestly, I'm worn out trying to keep up." Wow. Her family is trying to keep up with the proverbial Joneses, and all this time I thought they were the Joneses. She was in the chase like the rest of us. While others were chasing after the carrots she had, she was chasing after carrots someone else had. The carrots she possessed were nothing more than stage props. Once God allowed me a tiny peek behind the curtain of her life, I realized there was no blockbuster show in the making. Pastor Steven Furtick summed it up nicely in saying, "The reason we struggle with insecurity is because we compare our behind-the-scenes with everyone else's highlight reel."

A Lesson from Goldilocks

I'm embarrassed when I think back at my shallow thinking during that season of my life. I knew truth. I knew that happiness couldn't be bought or staged. I knew it could only be found in Christ and Christ alone. I even passed that truth along to my friend during our conversation. And she said she knew it too. But deep down inside, I knew there was a part of me that was still engaged in the chase.

Like Goldilocks in the classic fairy tale of our younger years, I was desperately searching for "just right." You remember the story. Goldilocks stumbles upon the three bears' house while she is taking a walk in the woods. She knocks on the door and, when no one answers, decides to let herself in and take a look around. (I believe we refer to that as "breaking and entering!") Upon her inspection of the bears' digs, she sees three bowls of soup on the kitchen table and decides to take a taste. The first bowl of porridge is too hot. The second bowl is too cold. But the third bowl is just right. She gobbles it up and then turns her attention to finding the perfect chair. She finally finds one that is just right, but when she sits on it, it collapses. Guess it wasn't just right after all.

She then moves on to the bears' bedrooms in a new quest to find the perfect bed. Searching for "just right" is exhausting, so a nap is in order. She finally finds a bed that is just right and falls fast asleep. Unfortunately, her nap was cut short when the three bears returned home. You know the rest of the story: Out goes Goldilocks—her just-right moment in her just-right bed after a just-right meal was interrupted by a just-now reality.

How many of us, like our friend Goldi, have the unhappy habit of peeking through someone else's windows in search of just right? Isn't that the irony of the carrot chase? The just right we long for always seems to be out of our grasp and in someone else's clutches. Why can't we be content with just now? Why can't we quit this nonsense of hopping from one bowl of porridge to another and be content with the bowl in front of us? Maybe, just maybe, God wants us to readjust our thinking and view *just now* as *just right*. Because the truth is, there is no such thing as just right.

If Only

The carrots we chase aren't always "stuff." Sometimes they are circumstances. Like a desperate desire to make the seventh-grade cheer squad. That was the first time I can recall playing the "if only" game. "If only I was a cheerleader, my life would be full and complete!" Oh sure, it sounds shallow now, but to a middle-school girl growing up in the heart of Texas, it was at the top of most every girl's list of adolescent dreams come true. Wearing the orange and white Travis Bobcat sweater and pleated skirt sealed your standing in the esteemed popular group. Boys would ask you to go steady. Girls would want to be your friend. And best of all, you would get out of school early for pep rallies and games. Being a cheerleader was at the top of the popularity food chain.

Over a hundred girls tried out in front of a panel of judges, each girl hoping to see her name listed among the fifteen girls. But that was only the first cut. The fifteen finalists would then advance to the next round where the final list of six would be determined by the student body. My best friend and I practiced after school during our sixth-grade year. I was overconfident going into tryouts because I was one of few girls who, at the time, had mastered a back handspring. And truth be told, I was already popular, so my biggest hurdle would be making it past the judges.

Tryout day finally arrived. I can still remember sitting on the gym floor in a cluster of girls, waiting to hear my name called as the cheer coach announced the fifteen finalists. My best friend's name was called. I waited anxiously, but my name was never called. I was devastated. Still to this day, I remember how hard it was to see the cheer squad practicing after school or performing at pep rallies and games. To make matters worse, I had to walk home from school alone since my best friend stayed after school for practice. I had tied my happiness to circumstances, and when they didn't play out as I had hoped, disappointment cast a long shadow on my entire seventh-grade year.

I set my sights on making the eighth-grade squad. Same carrot. New chase. Tryout day finally arrived, and this time my name was called. I advanced to the next round, threw a couple of back handsprings, and enough students circled my name on the ballot to put me on the squad. I finally seized the carrot. My best friend made the team too, so we hugged and pledged to be roomies at cheer camp. I remember thinking how happy I would be now that I was finally a cheerleader. But my happy dance didn't last long. The practices were long. Some of the girls were bossy. The sweater was itchy. The coach played favorites, and I wasn't one of them. And my best friend found a new best friend and roomed with her at cheer camp. I needed a new carrot to chase, and so the search continued.

As time goes on, the stakes get higher. Owning a pair of pom-poms in middle school is replaced with a new list of carrots in the "if only" pursuit. Maybe you've mumbled one or more of these:

If only . . . I could find a job.

If only . . . I could quit my job.

If only . . . I could find a husband.

If only . . . we could move out of this apartment and get a house.

If only . . . we could move out of this house and get a bigger house.

If only . . . I could potty-train my child.

If only . . . I could get pregnant.

If only . . . I could find a church.

If only . . . I could stay home with my kids.

If only . . . we could pay our bills.

If only . . . my husband hadn't left me.

If only . . . my child wasn't rebelling.

If only . . . my husband wasn't a porn addict.

If only . . . I didn't have such a tainted past.

If only . . . I could lose this weight.

If only . . . my husband was a believer.

A Slow Learner

In spite of the "if only" lesson I learned in my younger years, I continued to struggle with playing the "if only" game as I got older. I was particularly susceptible when the carrot involved my children's wants and desires. I recall a situation in which my daughter taught me a valuable lesson about the "if only" game. She was two weeks away from wrapping up first grade, and I told her she could have a friend in her class come over after school for a playdate. When I picked them up that afternoon, the two of them giggled most of the way home in the backseat of my car. As we were pulling into the neighborhood, I asked my daughter's friend if her family had any vacation plans for the summer. Big mistake. "Yes ma'am. We are going to go to Disney World and stay at the Disney resort." Ugh. My kids had been begging for years to go to Disney World! She continued, "And my mom said we get to eat breakfast with the Disney characters and go on a special tour of the Magic Kingdom Castle." Yay. Good for you, sweetie. OK, I didn't really say that out loud, but you can bet I was thinking it.

Remember my penny-watching husband? Yeah, so a Disney vacation was out of the question. In fact, just a few days prior, my husband had called a family meeting and announced that we were going to take a summer vacation to . . . drumroll, please . . . a state park in Arkansas! Woo-hoo. He then proceeded to lay out a bunch of pamphlets and allow each of the kids to pick a favorite activity to do during the trip.

My heart broke for what my little daughter must have been feeling as her friend rambled on about her upcoming vacation to Disney World. Ugh. If only . . . we could afford to take our kids to Disney World. If only . . . we could afford to stay at the Disney Resort. Let's face it; our entire trip to Arkansas was probably less than a day's worth of funnel cakes and Dippin' Dots at Magic Kingdom. And then, suddenly from the back seat, my daughter interrupted my little "if only" pity party and taught me a lesson I won't soon forget. "Well, guess where we're going?" she asked her friend in a tone of sincere wonderment. "We're going to Arkansas! And we're going to stay in a state park and go hiking every day. And my dad let us pick out the stuff we're going to do, so I picked digging for diamonds at this place called Crater of Diamonds. My older brother picked feeding the alligators at an alligator farm, and my younger brother picked horseback riding!"

As I glanced back in my rearview mirror, I saw my daughter's face light up as she wrapped up the Arkansas infomercial with, "I can't wait for summer!" And trust me, she couldn't. As we pulled into our driveway, I knew I'd just been schooled by a six-year-old. Oh, but the story gets even better. Her friend responded with, "Wooooooow. You are sooooo lucky. When I get home, I'm going to ask my mom if we can go to Arkansas this summer instead of Disney World." Oh, what I would have given to have been a fly on the wall for that scene! Folks, it's all about the presentation. It's about our attitudes, and mine clearly needed adjusting. My husband's excitement to make the most of our low budget summer vacation was contagious. Clearly, my daughter had caught the Arkansas bug. While I was busy feeling sorry for her for missing out on Disney World, she, in turn, was feeling sorry for her friend for missing out on Arkansas. For the record, my kids still talk about that trip to Arkansas.

Joyfully Ever After

Contentment is a character trait, and character traits are developed over the years by practice. When circumstances don't play out like we had hoped, we can choose to be content in the midst of our circumstances. James 1:2–3 reminds us, "Count it all joy, my brothers, when you meet trials of various kinds, for you know that the testing of your faith produces steadfastness." The Greek word for "joy" is *chara* (khar-ah´), which means "cheerfulness" or "calm delight." The Greek word for "steadfastness" is *hupŏmŏnē* (hoop-om-on-ay´), which means "cheerful (or hopeful) endurance," "constancy." Calm delight. Constancy. Where do I sign up? Joy, *chara*, is still around when the happy dance ends.

The pursuit of happiness is based on external circumstances. Joy and contentment come from an internal, settled peace that resides deep within our souls. That peace comes from looking to Jesus, the founder and perfecter of our faith, who for the joy (*chara*) that was set before him endured the cross (Heb. 12:2). It puts things into perspective when we think of Jesus demonstrating a "calm delight" in going to the cross to pay for sins he didn't commit. He was able to see past the moment of the cross and set his eyes on the long-term reward—being seated at the right hand of God. But let's not forget that he was human just like us. In the garden just prior to his crucifixion, he prayed, "My Father, if it be possible, let this cup pass from me" (Matt. 26:39 ESV). Ultimately, he forfeited happiness in the moment and for the joy set before him and endured the cross. "Nevertheless, not as I will, but as you will" (Matt. 26:39 ESV). We can put away our "if only" lists because, praise be to God, Jesus put away his.

One of the happiest days of my life was when I quit waiting for "happily-ever-after" to come find me and proclaimed joy in the *just now* season of life. And the next season. And the next. The problem with fairy tales is they always end where real life begins. Real life doesn't look like the fairy tales. Oh, we can gather up enough highlights to put together a montage of happy moments and make our lives *look* like a fairy tale if we really want to fool our audience. Sorry, but I'm over that game. When I think back at the story line of my own life, it's not the highlights that have made me who I am today.

It's the behind-the-scenes moments that have taught me the most about life and where true, lasting joy can be found. The behind-the-scene moments when my prefabricated gods failed to satisfy my fairy-tale expectations, and as a result, I found myself at the foot of the cross. The behind-the-scenes moments when my husband failed to "complete me," and in my disappointment, I found the only One who could. The behind-the-scenes moments when one of my children would stray from God's path, and I realized that I was powerless to make him/her return but not powerless to pray that God would go get them and bring them back. The behind-the-scenes moments when I wept over a severely fractured relationship with one of my parents but realized in the midst of my pain I had a Father who would never, ever forsake me. The behind-the-scenes moments when I didn't get the desires of my heart, only to realize it would have been a train wreck had I gotten them. The behind-the-scenes moments when I did get the desires of my heart, only to realize it still wasn't enough to satisfy a void in my heart that only Jesus could fill. The behind-the-scenes moments when I would slip up spiritually, and in my brokenness discover God's grace and mercy had not dried up. Life happens behind the scenes.

Hans Christian Anderson once wrote, "Every man's life is a fairy tale written by God's fingers." God holds the pen, but we determine the mood and tone of each chapter. It's time to let go of the fairy-tale expectations we once imagined for our lives. Happily-ever-after is a choice, not a prize offered to a chosen few who find the fairy tale. Let's quit chasing a temporary brand of happiness when joy can be ours today. True joy can only be found in Jesus Christ. Those who make him their pursuit will experience the greatest riches this earthly life has to offer. Better yet, the story doesn't end when the last page has been turned. It just keeps getting better and better. Why settle for a fairy-tale pipe dream when God has written us into the greatest story ever told—*his* story? Let us reflect daily on the beautiful love story of redemption. No fairy tale can match the rescue mission that took place in God's story. "But God shows his love for us in that while we were still sinners, Christ died for us" (Rom. 5:8 ESV). Our Prince awaits. Ever after . . . begins today.

Vicki's books, Bible studies, and information about inviting her to speak at your event can be found on her author website:

Also Available by Vicki Courtney

Also Available by Vicki Courtney

Vicki Courtney

the Virtuous Woman

shattering the superwoman myth